•Amy Beers•

INDIANAPOLIS BEER STORIES

History to Modern Craft in Circle City Brewing

AMERICAN PALATE

Published by American Palate
A Division of The History Press
Charleston, SC
www.historypress.com

First published 2022

Manufactured in the United States

ISBN 9781467144773

Library of Congress Control Number: 2022935425

To the ghosts of Indy's brewing past.
May you always haunt these pages.

And to the craft beer community.

CONTENTS

FOREWORD

Amy Beers's *Indianapolis Beer Stories* is a wink-wink-nod-nod page turner, a boon companion alongside the specialty chips bowl, a favorite craft beer within reach. Amy's perspective is to show "the who" in the Hoosier across Indianapolis's two-centuries story of brewers and patrons, as well as the connections that make for barstool "Didja know?"

Amy serves up a fast romp read, especially for new visitors to Circle City's brewpubs and other places where people gather to drink Indiana-made craft beverages. It's a selective catch up with how we got here and who's now brewing, along with why they dedicate their time and expertise on behalf of our pure delight in gathering for the greater good.

So, at home or on a barstool, crack open Amy Beers's Indy caseload of stories, and as always, please drink responsibly.

—RITA KOHN

ACKNOWLEDGEMENTS

I t's time to crack open a beer and celebrate this book! Here's a toast to everyone who's helped along the way. I couldn't have done this without you.

First and foremost, I'd like to thank Mike. You have been my rock. Thank you for all your love and support and for helping me stay sane through this massive project. I did it. I ate the elephant.

Thank you to my mother. Every word is there. I counted.

To Rita Kohn, your legacy shall not be forgotten for all you've done for the craft beer community. You have been an inspiration to me. Your support has meant the world.

Many thanks to Ron Smith and Anita Johnson for your support. Thank you for helping me make connections, for your time and for sharing your stories and photos.

I would also like to give many thanks to John Hill, Kwang Casey, Dave Colt, Clay Robinson, Eilise Lane, and Ray Kamstra for trusting me with your stories. It's been an honor.

I'd also like to thank Courtney and Abby of Guggman Haus, as well as Jason Wuerfel of Books and Brews, for sharing with me your stories. Fitting more than two hundred years of Indianapolis brewing history into a word limit was a challenge, and I'm sorry the more complete version didn't make the cut. Perhaps down the road I will tell it in another capacity.

Thank you to all the brewery owners and photographers who contributed photographs to share in the book, as well as to the staff members who helped coordinate interviews and gather photographs.

Acknowledgements

To the Millers of Greenfield, what a treat it was spending the afternoon viewing your collection. Thank you for taking the time, opening your home and allowing me to share such wonderful artifacts for the book. Thank you also to Dave Worthington for sharing your bottle collection and to Rands for helping. We didn't break anything!

I'd like to express my sincerest gratitude to all the library staff who helped me search every nook and cranny for facts and photographs—to the librarians of the Indianapolis Central Public Library, the Indiana Historical Society, the Indiana State Library, the IUPUI University Library, the Indiana State Archives and the St. Joseph County Public Library. Thank you to the Indiana Album, Indianapolis Motor Speedway, Current Publishing, the Indiana State Fairgrounds and the Brewers of Indiana Guild for sharing some of your collections.

To the beer writers, journalists and historians listed in the bibliography, thank you for the work you have done, the research and long hours spent in helping preserve this history. It has greatly aided in my own research.

I can't forget my brother in the acknowledgements. He explained sports to me in layman's terms and helped me write the sports bit in the Oaken Barrel chapter. I surely would have made a mess of it otherwise! I owe you a beer.

Special thanks and acknowledgements must go out to all the hardworking brewers who create magic in a glass, to my friends and followers who've been cheering me on and to the craft beer community. Without all of you, this would be nothing. This is your book.

And last but certainly not least, thank you to my publisher for giving me this incredible opportunity. To John Rodrigue for helping me through this process, my project editor Ryan Finn and the rest of the History Press staff.

Cheers!

INTRODUCTION

The president of a once great brewing empire haunts the last remaining testament to Indianapolis's beer legacy. A legacy long forgotten—a legacy paved by parking lots. To forget the story of brewing in Indianapolis is to forget Indianapolis. To disconnect from its past is to disconnect from the present. Erasing this heritage erases our collective identity.

Indianapolis Beer Stories: History to Modern Craft in Circle City Brewing brings that past to life. It circles back to connect the past with the present in a colorful presentation that is more of a narrative than a sequential reference book. Readers will delight in this collection of stories filled with adventure, drama, scandal, tears, laughter, hope and realized dreams.

This story isn't just about beer. It's more than a recitation of facts and figures, of brewing dates and barrel outputs. To tell the story of Indy's brewing history is to tell the story of Indianapolis—a contemporaneous relationship between how beer shaped the city and how the city shaped beer. It's a portrait of Indy's brewing pioneers both past and present. Moments captured in time tell of the dreamers, the movers and shakers, the spirited entrepreneurs, the risk takers, the innovators and passionate creators—the ones who thought outside the box, who rebelled against expectations, broke stereotypes and inspired by proving what could be. The ones who created history and those who continue to paint the picture for future generations are contained within this time capsule of stories.

The story begins with taverns, artisanal ales and the building up of a community. Readers will learn about Indy's isolation period, how new forms of transportation ushered commercial brewing into the new settlement. We see how a city fueled by beer grows during an industrial revolution and into a world-renowned center of trade that brings up brewing giants. The industry blooms into a turn-of-the-century golden era filled with innovation and internationally recognized brews. Then it buckles under its own weight as brewing monopolies dry up during Prohibition. We see an emergence from the dark into an even greater darkness riddled with attempts at filling the shoes of those gone before—a shell of what once was.

The second half of this book circles back to the emergence of a fresh, modern craft beer perspective, to the days of homebrewing and the artisanal brewery, to the essence of beer and the early taverns. That essence, the heart and soul of brewing, is all about community. It's about a space to gather and converse, a shared experience.

What a privilege and honor it was to have this opportunity to share the story of Indianapolis's brewing history with you and help preserve its legacy. I'm a Certified Cicerone who gives beer and brewery tours in Indianapolis through my company, Drinking with Beers. When I was asked to write this book and given a minimum and maximum word count, I thought to myself, *How am I going to fill an entire book focused solely on Indy's brewing history?* It seemed like a tall order. But as I scoured thousands of old newspapers, dug into old texts and interviewed some of today's key figures in craft beer, it became a different task: *How am I going to fit all of this rich history into one book?*

The Indianapolis beer community has a reputation to be proud of. I'm thrilled to be sharing these stories with you. I hope reading them fills you with as much wonderment and inspiration as I experienced writing them. And I hope, like with a good beer, you share this story with a friend over a pint.

• Part I •

History of Brewing in Indianapolis, 1820-1978

EARLY TAVERNS AND BREWERIES, 1820-1873

NOWLAND TO THE NEW LAND

Loaded with only the necessities for a journey into a perilous unknown, Elizabeth Byrne Nowland tucked her husband's famous Kentucky peach brandy next to the winter provisions inside the large, six-horse wagon. She bravely kissed the cheeks of her beloved entourage. Teary-eyed friends and family said goodbye in true southern fashion.

Miss Elizabeth was an admirable woman, loved by many, who became well known throughout Indiana. Despite being a quiet man who mostly kept to himself, Matthias R. Nowland won the love and affection of Miss Byrne. They married and lived in Frankfort, Kentucky. In 1820, they sold their generous estate and moved to Indianapolis, where they pioneered one of the town's first taverns.

Matthias was a successful, intelligent businessman. The year 1818 saw the signing of the New Purchase Agreement between the United States and the Miami, Delaware and Potawatomi indigenous tribes. It expanded Indiana's territory. In May 1820, commissioners gathered in Vincennes to begin their journey of locating and appointing a site for the new state capital. Nowland happened to be in the area, caught wind of this news and joined them.

They traveled up along the White River until they reached the mouth of Fall Creek. They stopped for a day and found that four or five families had come earlier that spring. As the commissioners explored the land, most became impressed with the territory. An optimistic Nowland saw tremendous business opportunity in a future new city. He convinced the commissioners to vote on that location. In turn, he agreed to return home and persuade his fellow Kentuckians to join him that coming fall. He also agreed to build a tavern to include sleeping quarters and an office for the new capital. Being one of the only men with means at the time, his wealth pulled a lot of weight. Thus, Nowland is often credited as having a large part in determining the location of Indianapolis.

There was much fear at the time surrounding the idea of uprooting to an unsettled wilderness. This period was marked with heightened tensions between settlers and natives. Despite pleadings from friends and family, the Nowlands stubbornly proceeded with their plans. The Nowlands' eldest son, John, who was about seven years old at the time, as he recalled in his *Early Reminiscences*:

> *They told him that he would never be permitted by the Indians to reach the White River, if he started; that he was endangering the lives of his whole family; in short, every argument was used to deter him from attempting so hazardous an undertaking; but all arguments were of no avail; his mind was made up the moment the selection of the site was made by the commissioners.*

Matthias finished hitching up the team of horses and loaded up their children for his family's journey to the new frontier. He waited for Elizabeth to say her final goodbyes. She mounted the horse prepared for her, politely sitting sidesaddle in her dress. John Nowland described saying goodbye to his nanny, who decided to stay behind out of fear. She fell to the ground on her knees in tears, praying for God to watch over them: "We left our home…to seek our fortune among strangers, in a wilderness whose population was almost entirely savage."

They left in October, waving goodbye to their friends and family as the morning fog enveloped their caravan. The distance between their past and future became greater each passing day. After a long, rugged journey, the family arrived in Indianapolis the following month on November 4, 1820. They joined a handful of about fifteen other families charting the newly acquired land.

The first settlers arrived to a thick, dense forest of large hardwood trees. They carved their way through the foliage, through spice bush and pawpaws, and built log cabins. On the opposite banks along the White River, one could see a scattering of wigwams and canoes. Stacks of smoke and the savory aroma of fresh game roasting over an open fire rose from the native tribal camps.

In the distance, along the east bank of the White River, on a narrow wedge of land about twenty-five to thirty feet above the water, sat John McCormick's cabin. It was a small cabin with little pens around it as sleeping apartments for guests. There is much debate over whether John McCormick or George Pogue was the first white man to settle in Indianapolis. The McCormick clan was of Irish descent. They came from the British colonies, from Pennsylvania and then Ohio, before settling in what would soon become Indiana's new capital. John McCormick arrived with his family in February 1820. They built the town's first tavern and boardinghouse.

In the early days, taverns played a key role in helping establish new settlements. They were the center of community, fostered economic growth and provided shelter and nourishment to travelers—a temporary housing solution for those not yet established. Cabins sometimes doubled as taverns. The first families to settle a new town often made it their duty to open their home for accommodation and entertainment. Visiting a tavern was an opportunity to socialize, exchange ideas and catch up on the latest town gossip. It provided an outlet for news and information from travelers who acted as a window to the outside world. It was a place for trade and commerce. Some taverns even functioned as a church or courthouse.

Taverns were also a common meeting place for government officials. As Senator Oliver H. Smith recounted in his *Early Indiana Trials and Sketches*, "It was universal custom of the judges and bar, to meet after supper, in some upper room of the tavern, and play cards and drink, sometimes till near morning." Taverns were a place to conduct business. In fact, McCormick's tavern served as the meeting location where the commissioners officially appointed the site for Indiana's permanent seat of government. Yes, the site for the new capital was perhaps decided over a pint of beer.

Beer was a common drink in those days, brewed partly out of necessity due to poor water conditions. The boiling part of the brewing process made water safe to drink. It was also nutritious and considered healthful for the whole family. Brewing beer was a domestic chore often handled by women. Although there is no hard evidence, it's likely that Elizabeth Nowland brewed beer for the family's tavern. It was located between Washington and Maryland Streets, west of Missouri Street.

Some early documented brewing recipes called for loaves with bran, wheat, hops, water, fresh yeast and sometimes the addition of various fruits, herbs and spices. As settlers traveled to new lands, they used resources available to them. Molasses, sassafras root and sometimes pumpkin became alternative ingredients. *Nowland's Early Reminiscences* talks of settlers drinking spruce beer. *Dunn's History* mentions the existence of porter in Indianapolis in the 1850s.

Matthias Nowland had a passion for sugar-making. He and his son John spent many nights at an old Native American sugar camp. It was located at the southeast end of Virginia Avenue (present-day Fountain Square Cultural District). Over the course of his sugar-making business, he produced more than six hundred pounds of sugar and a large quantity of the finest molasses. Perhaps Nowland's molasses was used in local beer recipes.

Nowland was also a skilled fisherman. He introduced hook-and-line fishing to the early Indianapolis settlers. Fish were plentiful and the water crystal clear. Sometimes there would be wagonloads of five-pound bass. He and John McCormick often went fishing together and supplied their taverns with the latest catch. Nowland also introduced the town's first watch. Everyone borrowed it to put marks on their doors for future use in estimating the time according to the sun's placement.

Although Nowland was a jack of all trades, his main occupation was masonry. He made the town's first kiln of brick. While working in his brickyard, he caught an illness. It claimed his life on November 11, 1822, just two years after the family's arrival to Indianapolis. He was thirty-five years old.

Before his death, he'd purchased several lots of land on deferred payment. A widowed Elizabeth became a single woman with five young mouths to feed. With little means of income, she forfeited the land. It left the family in poor financial condition. Elizabeth carried on by opening a boardinghouse in 1823. She was determined to keep her family together. She took out an advertisement in the *Indiana State Gazette* that read:

> *The undersigned respectfully informs the public that she has opened a house for private entertainment at her residence on Washington Street, nearly opposite Mr. Hawkin's Tavern; where she is prepared to accommodate all who may favor her with their custom, on as good terms and in as comfortable a manner as possible. She likewise continues to keep a boarding house, and returns her grateful acknowledgements for past favors, and intends still to supply her table with the best the country can afford, and hopes thereby to obtain liberal share of public patronage.*

She also designated one of her rooms as a general store. A bank took up residence in the front hall. With help from the community, she worked

CABIN OF MATTHIAS R. NOWLAND—A SCENE ON WASHINGTON ST., OCT. 9, 1821.

Cabin of Matthias R. Nowland. *From* Nowland's Sketches of Prominent Citizens.

tirelessly to support her children. She passed away in 1856. Her son, John, wrote of her, "No person who ever knew her could forget her universal good humor. In her kindness to all, both rich and poor, there was no distinction made in their treatment. The poor were never turned away hungry or empty handed from her door."

A City Built on Taverns

Nowland's tavern buzzed with a crowd of eager new settlers vying for plots of land in Indiana's new capital, Indianapolis. It was a soggy and scathingly windy autumn evening on October 8, 1821. There had been terrible floods, devastation of crops and considerable sickness that summer. But it did not deter the most ambitious of men. Beer flowed freely while competition, and prices, ran high.

Many had traveled hundreds of miles through unsettled wilderness by horse or ox-drawn wagon. They braved a rugged terrain in the hopes of a fresh beginning, to develop farmland or start businesses. They had immigrated to America from countries in northwestern Europe: England, Scotland, Ireland, Germany and France. Some brought their long history of brewing traditions.

Responding to advertisements for a new, developing city, settlers flocked to Nowland's tavern to buy land. Escaping from the harsh wind, those dreaming of a bright future crowded the tavern. The flickering light of the fire danced on the rustic tavern walls. The pleasant, sweet smell of spice and cider lingered in the air among the clamor of newcomers bidding for land.

The sale of this new land continued for a week and took place at various other taverns. The money from sales would eventually fund the statehouse, courthouse, governor's circle, the clerk's office of the Supreme Court, the treasurer's house and office and a ferryman's house at the foot of Washington Street.

The beginning of Indianapolis was marked by a strong sense of hope and community. The early settlers bonded together in support of a shared goal. They were building a new life in a new city. John Nowland recalled their first Christmas in *Early Reminiscences*:

> *About four o'clock, Christmas morning, we were awakened by a salute from eight or ten rifles, and the cry of "Get up, Kaintuck; we want some of that old peach brandy"…of which they had drank freely while building our cabin. When he opened the door, the entire male portion of the Harding and McCormick population stepped into the cabin, and gave three cheers for "Old Kaintuck, the new-comer." After paying the brandy the highest compliment in their power by drinking freely of it, they went to and saluted the inmates of the different cabins in a similar way. There was no petty jealousy in the people at that day; all seemed on an equality…as members of one common family.*

As the town grew, so did the need and demand for taverns. Shortly after Nowland built his tavern in 1821, Major Thomas Carter built the pretentious Rosebush Tavern. It sat in front of his original tavern between

Washington and Market Streets, just east of Illinois. John Nowland described the one-and-a-half-story framed building as having a "very imposing appearance."

Samuel Rooker, a local artist, painted the tavern sign. It was modeled after those found in England. Carter's glorious tavern sign depicted a rosebush. It stood on a tall post in front of the tavern, swinging back and forth in old-country fashion. A.C. Howard's historical sketch described it as "rude."

Carter built another tavern in 1823 moving Rosebush to a new location across from the courthouse on Washington Street. The sign went with it. The new tavern was described as "a hotel of more pretentious character than its log predecessor." The town's first Baptist sermon was held there. It was also the site of the first recorded fire in Indianapolis. All hell broke loose, and the tavern burned to the ground on January 17, 1825, during the first session of the legislature. The fire started from a keg of ashes at about nine o'clock that night. Some of the town's men ran to the site in a panic, hoping to save the treasured Rosebush sign from encroaching flames. They began chopping down the post like a tree. It fell, but the sign splintered into pieces, rendering it completely and utterly destroyed. An unstoppable Major Carter pressed on.

That spring, he purchased the city's first two-story framed house near West Street. It boasted a very commodious space of eighteen by twenty feet. He moved it to his Washington Street location, replacing the burned-down Rosebush Tavern. The whole process took several weeks. It caused quite a disruption from the debris of stumps and logs. Carter continued to prosper at this tavern.

A man of distinction, Mr. Carter did well to avoid frivolities, except for drinking. Even so, he was a man of moderation. Described as a "forty-gallon Baptist," he found drinking more acceptable than engaging in song and dance. But if there were anything he despised most, it was the fiddle. He loathed the fiddle and "thought the devil incarnate lay in the bowels of one. Under no circumstances would he allow one about his house."

One day, a traveling Parisian entertainer by the name of Monsieur Crampton paid Indianapolis a visit. It was the winter of 1825–26. Hoping to bestow on the townspeople an evening of entertainment and seeing that Mr. Carter's tavern was the only building large enough to host such a performance, Crampton requested the use of Carter's dining room.

Carter was hesitant on allowing such a performance, as he was well aware that these types of entertainments often included music on the fiddle. Crampton reassured Carter that he hated the fiddle as much as he and promised only to play the violin. With this, Carter allowed the city's first theatrical performance.

Nearly everyone in Indianapolis crammed shoulder to shoulder into the dining hall, waiting to watch Crampton play a well-known and beloved character known as Bill Bagwell. The low murmur of guests slowly came to silence. The doors opened. Poised with a fiddle resting on his shoulder and bow in hand, Bagwell began playing vigorously. The tune of "Leather Breeches," however, soon came to a sudden halt. A once smiling crowd turned their heads in confusion to see why the joyous song had stopped.

There stood a stern Major Carter, cane in hand, demanding Mr. Crampton desist his fiddle playing at once. According to *Nowland's Early Reminiscences*, the conversation went like this:

> *"But Monsieur," explained Crampton, "you are mistaken. For this is my violin I brought with me from Paris."*
>
> *"No," replied Carter, "I can't be mistaken, for Bill Bagwell can't play on anything else than a fiddle."*
>
> *Getting back into the character of Bagwell, Crampton assured him, "Major, just bring in a bottle of Bayou Blue and see how I'll play on it. You are mistaken, Major; this is nothing but a violin."*

Unconvinced but seeing the crowd of people at his tavern, Carter permitted the playing of the fiddle, but *only* as long as Bagwell played Psalm tunes and *only* Psalm tunes. Carter was certain that Bagwell didn't know any Psalm tunes. Much to his surprise, Bagwell foiled Carter's clever plan because he was, in fact, a member in good standing at the Baptist church. He began playing "Jesus My All to Heaven Is Gone." This tickled Carter's fancy. The evening's entertainment on the *fiddle* continued well into the night, closed by request to the tune of "Yankee Doodle."

In the same year as Nowland and Carter, John Hawkins opened Eagle Tavern on the north side of Washington Street between Meridian and Pennsylvania. It served as the town's first post office. This double log cabin was built from the trees on the land where it stood. The trees were so dense that if you stood in the doorway of the tavern, you wouldn't be able to see someone across the road half a block away. Hawkins had also commissioned Samuel Rooker to paint his tavern sign, but the eagle turned out to look more like a turkey. Years later, a wild turkey was shot on the rooftop of Hawkins's tavern.

Several other taverns opened as the population of Indianapolis increased, with some worthy of note. Partners James Blake and Samuel Henderson, the latter being the first mayor of Indianapolis, opened a tavern in 1824. It once hosted a small traveling circus that included elephants. Mr. Blake sold the tavern to Mr. Henderson, who kept the tavern until 1835, when he sold it to Washington Hall Company. It added an addition, and although it changed hands several times, Washington Hall was always known as a first-class hotel in Indianapolis and the best in Indiana.

In the 1850s, J.W. Canan opened the Tremont House on Illinois Street near Union Station. He saw much success because of the tavern's prime location near the railways. Union Station in Indianapolis was an innovative railway system. It allowed for a level of convenience not yet experienced in the travel industry. Allegedly, the tavern also served as part of the Underground Railroad, as there was a secret tunnel connected to the station.

Mr. Canan entertained many wealthy travelers until the 1860s, when the Tremont House became the Concordia House. It was the first German American club of Indianapolis and later renamed the Germania House. It became Moore's Beer Tavern when it changed ownership just before Prohibition. During Prohibition, it became Moore's "Restaurant" and made alcoholic beverages in the basement. The tavern has had a long history,

Old Tavern on East Washington Street. *Indiana Historical Society, P0411.*

with many owners. Today, it is the oldest continuously operated tavern in Indiana. Locals know it as a popular and nationally recognized bar with live blues music called the Slippery Noodle.

Taverns were the building blocks of Indianapolis's history. They helped create a sense of community, providing the early townspeople and visitors alike with a place to eat, drink and be merry. As the city grew, so did the demand for beer. The first brewery, however, wouldn't emerge until 1834.

FULL STEAM AHEAD

Dozens of flatboats dotted along the White River navigated strenuously along its winding route, loaded with local produce, large assortments of merchandise and other household provisions. Some carried loads of flour, bacon, salt and whiskey. Others were burdened with heavy loads of corn, wheat and oats—some likely to be used for brewing beer. Much of the dense forest surrounding the river had been cleared to make room for farms. Cattle and hogs grazed among recently cultivated fields, offering forth the aromas of earth. Rustic log cabins lined the riverbanks, joined by water-powered gristmills. The Bayou Mills and Distillery, the first distillery of Indianapolis and famous for its "Bayou Blue" whiskey, could be seen on the west side of the river. Farther still was John McCormick's tavern, situated high on the bank.

Until the first roads and railways, waterways were a major source of transportation in early America. They acted as public highways. The White River was essential to Indianapolis's growing agricultural industry. In fact, the site for the new state capital was chosen after serious consideration of the waterways. However, the river later proved less navigable than initially expected, as it was too shallow most of the year. The roads that did exist were of terrible condition. They consisted mostly of cow paths and traces riddled with mud. A small window of opportunity for travel by wagon was confined to the colder months, when the ground was stiff from frigid temperatures.

As a result, Indianapolis remained a small, isolated settlement for much of its early years. Many who made the long, arduous expedition had not anticipated such slow growth and began to feel disheartened. With little contact with the outside world, settlers relied on one another and their own resources. Taverns remained the centers of community. There was no need, nor a large enough population, to support a brewery of any considerable scale. But slowly, circumstances began to change. The seat of state government officially moved from Corydon to Indianapolis in 1825. Effort toward improving the White River attempted to make it more navigable. A brewery was just on the horizon.

A gray mist loomed over the clear, glassy river. It dissipated from the rising sun to reveal the morning dew glistening among the grassy fields. Flatboats gathered in the waters. As the sun rose to grace the tops of the highest tree branches, a curious-sounding horn echoed in the distance, announcing a coming presence.

Paddling gloriously through the mist came the *Robert Hanna* steamboat. It passed rapidly by the flatboats as the men stopped to stare. It cut effortlessly through the river, its paddle wheel rhythmically splashing through the water, leaving behind a trail of lively white waves in its wake. Its smokestacks filled the crisp air with the coal-burning smell of an industrial revolution. It was a moment of celebration, for no other steamboat was able to successfully ascend the river to Indianapolis.

Before the *Robert Hanna*'s momentous arrival, a few steamboats had made the attempt the year prior, enticed by a handsome cash reward offered by Governor Noble. He was convinced that the route was still capable of extensive navigation, and he wanted to prove it. Some steamboats got close but never made it all the way to the capital. Finally, after some difficulty, the steamboat navigated under General Robert Hanna arrived to Indianapolis on April 11, 1831.

Everyone was overjoyed. A committee, including tavern owner Samuel Henderson, met to "make arrangements to demonstrate, in some appropriate manner, the high gratification which is and should be felt by all who feel interested in our commercial and agricultural prosperity." An exhilarated crowd of townspeople gathered along the riverbank to behold the proud triumph. At two o'clock, a parade of artillery marched to the river near the boat. They fired a cannon and a several rounds salute in honor of the occasion. Editors of the *Indianapolis Journal* claimed, "No event is recollected since the first settlement of this town, which produced a higher excitement."

However, the proud triumph came to a crashing halt—literally. The next morning, the *Robert Hanna* smashed into an overhanging tree. The force was so strong that it knocked down the pilothouse and chimneys. Frightened passengers jumped into the river for their lives. The next day, it started back up the river but got stuck on an island for six weeks. This ended steamboat navigation in that part of White River until 1865.

When *Robert Hanna* arrived in Indianapolis from Cincinnati that spring of 1831, it brought with it a load of stone and timber for the National Road bridge

Above: Steamboat *Governor Morton* docked near Wernweg's Bridge. *Indiana State Library.*

Opposite: William Wernweg's National Road Bridge over White River, Indianapolis. *St. Joseph County Public Library.*

at Washington Street. It also brought a band of contractors to help build the road through Indianapolis. Included was William Wernweg, contractor for the bridge. He would later build the town's first brewery.

The National Road was the first major improved highway built by the federal government. It played a key role in westward migration. Construction of the road through Indianapolis began in 1828. Running east to west, the 156-mile stretch across Indiana is currently known as U.S. 40 and locally as Washington Street. The road brought greater connectivity. It attracted a labor force and increased the city's population. Prospects of new business and industry developed. It paved the way for a future brewing industry.

Wernweg began construction for Indy's National Road bridge the summer of 1831. After he completed his work in 1834, he established a small brewery with business partner, John L. Young. The brewery would later become known as the Indianapolis Brewery. It was located west of an

NATIONAL ROAD BRIDGE. *Over White River, Indianapolis.* SERIES 1. NO. 14. M. R. HYMAN, PUBLISHER, INDIANAPOLIS

anticipated Indiana Central Canal on the south side of Maryland Street, between West and Missouri.

Indianapolis continued with steady growth. The Mammoth Improvement Act of 1836 created plans for city infrastructure. Projects included the addition of turnpikes, canals and, later, railroads. But just as hope began to reach full bloom in an awakened Indianapolis, a financial crisis hit the United States in 1837 that touched off a major recession. Construction intended to connect the Central Canal in Marion County to the state's other canals, as well as plans for railroads, was abandoned in 1839.

The town was devastated. Dreams were shattered. People began to leave. In 1838, the estimated population of Indianapolis was 4,000. People had estimated that it would double in five years. But by 1840, the population was only 2,662. Indiana was close to bankruptcy. The Improvement Act became one of the greatest debacles in the history of the state. The National Road through Indianapolis did not prove to be as stimulating for new business. Although taverns continued hosting travelers along the road, early attempts at a manufacturing industry failed.

Wernweg and Young's brewery pressed on for a short time. They sold the brewery sometime around 1840 to an energetic and industrious Frenchman by the name of Joseph Laux. Laux came to Indianapolis during the Panic of 1837 with his wife, Josephine. They were a wealthy and generous couple. Nowland's *Sketches of Prominent Citizens* described Mrs. Laux as a "hospitable and charitable lady, contributing freely for all benevolent purposes." Mr. Laux was of high moral character—an honest man who bought grain from the local farmers, drank his own beer and sold yeast to housewives for home bread baking. He never troubled anyone, except for when he wanted frog legs, for which he bartered with the neighborhood boys in exchange for beer.

Laux carried on with the Indianapolis Brewery for a few years before moving his business across town, near the east end of the National Road on the corner of Noble (current College) and Washington Streets. There, he developed a partnership with Frederick H. Brandt in 1846. In 1849, their partnership dissolved. About a month later, Laux took out an ad in the newspaper with the heading "Temperance and Whiskey" with a wish to dispose of his "Still" and "Apparatus." The following month, in an alleged accident, a faulty kiln ignited a fire. It consumed the whole brewery and completely destroyed Laux's newly purchased supply of grain.

Research did not turn up whether or not Laux was able to resume brewing operations; however, an 1857 directory listed a Charles Ghuss brewery at the same location of Laux's brewery on east Washington. There was no record of Laux. There *is* record in the same directory of a Joseph *Loucks* near that same location. He owned a shop and was listed as a cooper, a person who makes wooden casks, barrels, vats, buckets, tubs, troughs and similar containers. The shop was likely an extension of the brewery, and perhaps the two were partners.

After Laux left the original Wernweg & Young brewery around 1842, Christian Hepp and August Joachimi took over the site. Their partnership dissolved in 1847. Joachimi continued the business. An article in the *Indiana State Sentinel* reads, "He will keep constantly on hand a superior and healthy article of strong beer and ale. Also, fresh yeast."

At some point, Joachimi ceased his brewery business, and many sources point to John P. Meikel as being the one who continued the operation. The earliest Indianapolis directory, dated 1855, lists Meikel as a brewer at the Maryland Street location (Wernweg's former brewery). Meikel stated in a newspaper article dated 1865 that he'd been in the brewing business for fifteen years. I would surmise that Meikel probably started brewing at the Indianapolis Brewery in 1850. Whether he took over operations that year or was brewing as an apprentice and later became owner is unclear. An 1862 newspaper article stated, "J.P. Meikel, proprietor, is now turning out a magnificent article of beer. It is a splendid spring-time drink."

Sketch of Meikel's Brewery and residence on Maryland Street—the first Indianapolis brewery. *Indiana State Library.*

There were many breweries that opened between 1834 and 1869. Most faced a tremulous start and didn't last long. Meikel was the first of the early brewers to experience success and longevity. He emigrated from Germany and came to Indianapolis from Cincinnati sometime in 1840. He would have been about nineteen years old. Meikel became known as *the* Indianapolis brewer. His brewery was lovingly remembered by locals as "The Old Brewery."

A RISE AND FIGHT FOR BEER

A newfound hope came to Indianapolis with the advent of the town's first railroad in 1847. The railway connected Indianapolis to Madison, an Indiana boomtown located advantageously next to the Ohio River. The new rail line created a gateway to commerce and began to increase Indy's potential for a brewing industry. By 1850, there were five railway lines, bringing the town an economic boost with increased trade and new jobs. It was finally the end of isolation.

Indianapolis was the first city in the world to devise a union station. It opened in 1853 and connected multiple rail lines. This new system significantly transformed travel and industry. Word spread regarding the highly acclaimed rail system, and Indianapolis adopted the nickname "The Railway City." Union Station caused a dramatic shift in commercial activity. By 1863, Indianapolis had become a bona fide center for wholesale trade. People came in droves to a city bursting with new opportunity.

Indianapolis Union Station, 1920. *Indiana Historical Society, P0062.*

In 1848, Indianapolis saw an influx of German immigrants escaping the aftermath of a failed revolution. Other waves came by offer of free land through Homestead Acts. Many Germans brought considerable wealth and were educated and highly skilled. Growing cities looking to further develop their economy often encouraged these Germans to settle there. In Indianapolis, they contributed greatly to architecture, education, politics, the arts, agriculture and, of course, brewing. In fact, German Americans founded many, if not most, of Indiana's first breweries.

Escaping difficult circumstances, many people came from Ireland to Indianapolis to work on the canals, railways and roads. The Irish Potato Famine had left their homeland faced with disease and mass starvation. Others had been pushed off their farms during a massive industrialization movement, deprived of the means to earn a living.

By 1860, there were nearly 4,000 native-born Germans living in Indianapolis, making up 60 percent of the city's foreign population. The second-largest group were the Irish at more than 1,700 native born, representing about 26 percent. In total, Indianapolis grew to a population of more than 18,000 residents.

Germany and Ireland are famous for their beer culture. The Germans, especially, have a long, illustrious relationship with beer. They are most noted for their crisp, sparkling lagers that remain a worldwide favorite. Ireland introduced the world to Guinness.

Indianapolis had proven itself as a major transportation hub, and this attracted new business, industry, job opportunities and a subsequent population boom. Demand rose from a new culture of beer aficionados and a labor force that often drank beer. Conditions for a more serious brewing industry finally began to take shape. However, temperance movements were also on the rise.

Before Prohibition of the 1920s, with its underground speakeasies, came Indiana's "mini-prohibition" of 1855. The Indiana Temperance Society formed in 1830, and local temperance societies soon organized in Indianapolis. Temperance groups blamed crime, poverty, domestic abuse and immorality on alcohol and drunkenness. Many believed that the answer to this problem was complete abstinence. Concerned with the moral fabric of society, reformers announced that "the devil was at work and must be repudiated." They believed that if they could control alcohol consumption, they could restore morality.

By the 1850s, the Know-Nothing Party had formed and was bolstering the temperance movement. The group consisted mostly of middle-class Protestants with strong anti-Catholic and anti-immigrant sentiments. Fueled mainly by xenophobia, they perceived a connection between the "foreign element" and the brewing industry.

Discrimination began to boil toward Irish immigrants, as some sources described the group's proclivity for drinking and rowdiness. Many owned saloons. Germans especially began to dominate the brewing industry. There was also concern with job loss to immigrants. The Know-Nothing Party sought to decrease foreign influence by prohibiting brewing and alcohol.

Its support of temperance societies, along with the Republican Party, helped pass a statewide prohibition law in Indiana. It went into effect on June 12, 1855. It prohibited the manufacture and sale of spirits, including beer, wine, cider and all other fermented beverages—except for medicinal, chemical, mechanical and religious purposes. It authorized designated county agents the right to purchase however much alcohol was needed from those specially licensed to manufacture it. They could then resell it (at a fixed cost) for the permitted uses. These agents were appointed under the law, supplied with funds from the county treasury and compensated for their services. Any profits they acquired were owed to the county treasury. While these agents were permitted to purchase booze from local manufacturers, they were "not required to do so, and as a matter of fact do not, but obtain them in most cases from abroad," for which exception was made because imports could not be prohibited under U.S. law.

Riots broke out as authorities attempted to shut down saloons. Many remained open in defiance. One man in particular resisted. On July 2, 1855, Roderick Beebe, who owned the famous and high-end Empire Saloon on Washington Street, refused to cease his operation. In a statement of defiance, he openly continued selling beer. He was fined fifty dollars, which he refused to pay, and was imprisoned for his rebellion.

Beebe soon obtained the writ of habeas corpus, and the county court ruled him guilty. He then appealed to the state Supreme Court. Judge Perkins, who was opposed to the new liquor law, discussed the matter thoroughly with his colleagues. There were disagreements. The case dragged on until November, when another saloonkeeper, named Herman, was arrested on similar charges.

They brought Herman before Judge Perkins. His attorney proposed to submit the case under the same argument prepared for Beebe. After a lengthy discourse regarding the merits of the law and reviewing the previous arguments, Judge Perkins deemed the law unconstitutional. He stated the legislature could not completely prohibit the liquor business nor the right of an individual to select what he or she chose to eat or drink. The conviction, therefore, was invalid.

The decision was made at two o'clock that afternoon. Word spread quickly to every town and every telegraph line in the state. Upon Beebe and Herman's release, the saloon doors were flung open. A flood of drunken excitement filled the streets. According to the *Indiana Magazine of History*, there were more drunks in Indiana five hours after the decision than there had been during the entire five months of the existence of the prohibition law. Meanwhile, a sad and defeated crowd of sober temperance societies looked on from a distance. Decades of hard work were lost in what seemed like an instant: "But in spite of all these great misfortunes, [temperance supporters] were able to keep alive that little spark of divine inspiration.…Things might hinder them for the time being yet in the future they could go forth to battle again."

The Civil War, fought primarily for the emancipation of enslaved African Americans in the southern Confederate States, was just around the corner. As much as temperance supporters fought their prohibition case, the federal government needed tax dollars to fund the Union army of the northern states. A good portion of that money came from beer.

President Lincoln signed the Revenue Act of 1862. This included a tax on the manufacture and sale of "all beer, lager beer, ale, porter, and other similar fermented liquors, by whatever name such liquors may be called." The excise tax on beer was one dollar per thirty-one-gallon barrel. The average cost per barrel was about four to five dollars—a pretty hefty tax! Many supporters of the Union considered the tax patriotic. Beer sales throughout the war increased. In 1860, 8 million barrels of beer were sold. By the end of the war in 1865, the annual output had increased to 24 million. Indeed, beer played an important role in funding the war. But as soon as the war ended, temperance societies were back at it, striking at any opportunity.

In August 1865, there was a sudden and discriminatory denial of liquor licenses in Indianapolis. It created much excitement among the liquor interests. Leaders extended an invitation to "all who could drink a glass of beer or wine without making beasts of themselves, and who were opposed to fanaticism." About two hundred people joined the meeting. Attendance consisted of native-born Americans and German immigrants as well as a fair number of temperance men. A portion of the meeting was spoken in German.

A Mr. Newkirk addressed the uproarious gathering of Indianapolis men involved in the liquor business, according to the *Daily State Sentinel*: "Now that the war is past, and there is nothing to fight over…some people must find some pretext for throwing stones at their neighbors, even if they did live in big glass houses themselves. The temperance men must fight something, and they might as well fight the liquor interest."

Newkirk gave a speech appealing to both the liquor interests and the temperance supporters. Some discreditable liquor dealers operated in shady business, making a bad name for the industry. He encouraged those involved in the manufacture and sale of alcohol to do so under the provisions set forth in the law, so as not to create an attitude of fanaticism among temperance societies.

The opposition came from temperance reformers filing remonstrances to the Board of County Commissioners. One liquor license denial was made against longtime brewery owner John P. Meikel. He was a German immigrant. Much to Meikel's surprise, his renewal was denied on the grounds that he "is immoral and unfit to be trusted with such license," noted the *Daily State Sentinel*.

The next day's *Sentinel* saw a strongly worded letter delivered by the respectable Mr. Meikel:

> *To the Public:*
> *I would state that I have been a citizen of Indianapolis for near thirty years, and I challenge proof of any acts of immorality on my part. I have been in the brewery business fifteen years and this is the first time a charge has been made against me as a person "unfit to be trusted with a license" for the prosecution of my business. When such charges as these are made against a citizen for no other cause than to gratify a spirit of fanaticism, which prompts men to interfere in the business of their neighbors, and to slander and vilify, to make their cause good, it is time that a remedy should be applied so potent in its character as to teach meddlers that character cannot be maligned with impunity.*

Indiana men with beer. *Indiana Historical Society, P0611.*

Then Meikel boldly called out the attorney on the case:

> *In charity to the attorney, Mr. Fishback, who prosecuted the case for the temperance men, I would be willing to believe that he was not aware of the meaning of the word "immoral," and would ask him to come to my brewery, where he can learn from Webster's Dictionary what it conveys.*

The board granted Meikel his license, and he continued with the brewery. But it was not the end in the fight for prohibition. Temperance movements would rise once again to wreak havoc on the imbibers of tomorrow. For now, the city's emerging beer industry was in business. The fog lifted and the dust settled. A handful of new breweries opened in the wake of the 1855 repeal, some during the Civil War, and several would see the glorious era of Indy's golden age of brewing.

THE FIRST WAVE

The soldier removed his dark-blue kepi, wiped the sweat from his brow, cracked open a bottle of Schmidt's lager and joined his fellow comrades for a few beers. The crisp, sweet malt taste and zing from the hops felt cool and refreshing in the summer heat. He surveyed the camp, his temporary home. Wind blew through the stark white tents, kicking up dirt and dust in its path.

Indianapolis was a major military hub for the Union army and saw several camps established at the start of the Civil War in 1861. Because of the centralized location amid wartime camaraderie, the city experienced another rapid increase in population. Coupled with the fact that the beer tax for the war included expression of patriotism by quaffing down a few pints, demand for beer increased.

The population of Indianapolis grew from eight thousand in 1850 to more than forty-five thousand by the end of 1864. A once-quiet town was now abuzz with activity, a center for wholesale trade. Satisfying the increased demand for beer required more breweries, and many rose to the opportunity.

Late nineteenth-century breweries were not like today's craft breweries. Existing more as beer factories, they manufactured beer on a mass-produced, commercial scale. They operated as wholesalers and often distributed beyond local boarders. These brewing companies would also own and lease retail space for distribution. They would financially support saloons, taverns and beer gardens under certain terms and conditions that required them to sell their beer. This business model was, and continues to be, a traditional system of some European countries, especially Germany. Tied houses, as they were called, helped guarantee a sales outlet. It would be unlikely to find customers bellied up to a bar inside the brewery. Some breweries did establish an on-premises bar, but it was reserved for employees only. Brewing companies had separate bottling facilities or contracted out to bottling companies, as was required by law. Proprietors rarely worked as brewers. Instead, they focused their attention to overseeing the business.

Brewing was on the rise in Indianapolis. An 1857 city directory saw the addition of Charles Ghuss's Brewery at College (then Noble) and Washington Streets. There was also a listing and an advertisement that same year for Charles Augustus Imbery's Boarding House, Lager Beer Brewery and Summer House on the west side of the Madison railway depot.

The next year, Henry Buscher was listed on the corner of Pearl and Alabama, between Washington and Maryland. Partners George Dietz and Jacob Hill opened a brewery along the National Road. The two later split.

C.F. Schmidt Bottle. *Dave Worthington Collection.*

Frank Wright's Ale. *Dave Worthington Collection.*

Dietz left to operate Washington Hall Saloon. A French wine-dealer and brewer by the name of Adolph Jacquet took over in 1860.

In either 1859 or 1860, business partners Christian Frederick Schmidt and Charles Jaeger opened a brewery on McCarty Street, between Alabama and New Jersey. Then, around the start of the Civil War in 1861, brewers Frederick and Henry Harting founded the Harting Brothers Brewery. It was located on Bluff Road (begins on South Meridian) near McCarty Street and close to Schmidt's.

The following year, Frank Wright opened a brewery with business partner W.S. Downer. It was located on Blake Street near a mill, between New York and Ohio Streets on the current IUPUI campus. They brewed Downer's champagne ale. Then, in 1864, it seems that Downer dropped out of the game. It became Frank Wright's brewery and was later named Capital Brewery. Most breweries at the time brewed "common beer." According to *Sulgrove's History*, Wright was the first in Indianapolis to brew ale. But the brewery closed in 1876, after his ales surrendered to the popularity of lagers. Wright was also a dealer in oysters and canned fruits.

There was a Gagg & Company, first referenced in *Buell and Williams' Indianapolis City Directory and Business Mirror* for 1864. Later sources refer to the same as the Gack & Biser Brewery. According to the *Encyclopedia of Indianapolis*, the brewery was founded in 1859 and was purchased by Peter Lieber in 1863. However, current research does not turn up any evidence to support that finding. No directories listed a "*Gack* and Biser" brewery. It appears that a Rudolph *Gagg* and Peter Lieber were in business together. They were listed under Gagg & Company and operated as City Brewery beginning in 1864. The brewery was located on South Pennsylvania Street between South and Merrill near Madison Avenue.

Casper Maus began brewing with his son Albert, George Kalb and their neighbor on Alabama Street, Henry Buscher in 1865. Casper Maus and Kalb soon formed Casper Maus & Company. In 1867, they went their separate ways. Kalb continued brewing at another location for a short while. By 1868, Maus had moved across town and started a new brewery at the west end of New York Street near Frank Wright's brewery. It was located on the northwest corner where New York meets current University Boulevard. The last of the breweries to open in that first wave was Conrad Sponsel and Peter Balz's Union Brewery in 1869.

Circumstances seemed to be looking up in the birth of Indy's Wholesale District. The city's brewing industry had come a long way since Wernweg's brewery in 1834. But unfortunately, the first brewing wave would crash against the Financial Panic of 1873. Just as a beer scene finally emerged, another nationwide recession hit. Many breweries closed. A few, however, continued to thrive. They would later go on to become brewing legends, bottling a legacy not soon forgotten by brewery aficionados.

What ever became of John Meikel's Old Indianapolis Brewery? Meikel continued plugging along during the tumultuous era surrounding the temperance movements of the 1850s. In 1867, he purchased the Carlisle House and transferred his brewery there. It was located about a block northwest from the original brewery, on the corner of Washington and (at the time) California. Hotels next to the White River currently exist there.

The Carlisle House was built as a hotel in 1848, taking advantage of the city's new Madison railway line. Although it was a popular destination among travelers, it soon succumbed to competition from the famous Washington Hall and Union Hotel. It devolved into a dilapidated, fourth-rate tavern with a basement saloon kept by an owner who facetiously called it the "Cottage of Content."

Meikel also worked in real estate development. He helped build a neighborhood that would later be designated as Ransom Place. This current historic district is the most intact nineteenth-century neighborhood associated with African Americans in Indianapolis. Many prominent and influential citizens lived there.

With his expertise, Meikel spent a year remodeling the old Carlisle Hotel into a brewery. It was powered by steam and was the largest in Indianapolis at the time, located about a mile south of Ransom Place. He did a good amount of business at this new location. Meikel became one of the wealthiest citizens in the city and was very generous to his neighbors. He lived in a neighborhood enclave for Irish, German and Jewish immigrants.

It was located about a mile south of his brewery. Because of its location on the south side of Indianapolis, many African Americans called that neighborhood home after the Civil War's Emancipation Proclamation in 1863.

A man of community, Meikel often helped his neighbors pay their debts. His selflessness, unfortunately, led to his own detriment, as he became swept up in the unanticipated Financial Panic of 1873 and lost the brewery. G.F. Adams bought the brewery on foreclosure for $6,500. In the summer of 1875, parties negotiated for a fresh new start for Meikel's brewery. Whether they were trying to help their friend Meikel or start an unrelated brewery of their own is unclear. Perhaps some kindly citizens were trying to return a favor. These plans, however, did not come to fruition.

Interestingly, later that autumn, there were several attempts to burn down the building. Were the parties involved trying to collect insurance money after realizing that their investment wouldn't turn a profit? Or perhaps it was delinquent youths looking for trouble. Maybe it was a troubled Meikel.

Many years later, the old brewer suffered a curious and disastrous fall. In the middle of the night, Meikel arose from his bed. He stumbled to the second-story window and opened it. Positioning himself, he stepped out onto the roof of a shed located two feet below and lost his balance. He rolled to the ground. The loud *thud* of his body meeting the earth startled his family awake. They ran outside to see about the matter and found him unconscious in the dirt with a broken hip. Physicians determined that he suffered other internal injuries and would be unable to recover. Slipping in and out of consciousness, Meikel could not recall exactly what had happened.

He passed away five years later in 1886 at the age of sixty-five. At the time, he was one of the city's oldest remaining of the original Germans. Upon his death, he left behind a valuable estate. His family donated some of the land for Meikel Street Park, named in his honor. The name of the park has since been changed to Babe Denny Park, renamed to honor a longtime Parks Department employee. It's located at the corner of Meikel Street and Wyoming, in the shadow of Lucas Oil Stadium.

As far as the old brewery, it survived the incendiary attempts but never revived its brewing operations. Adams remodeled it into a tenement house, far removed from its former glory days as a luxury hotel. An eyesore of its remains. Various owners sublet the space, the rooms being divided into smaller and smaller units. Families were shoved into six-by-seven-foot rooms. The building became known as the "Home for the Friendless." It was condemned in 1882. An inspection deemed it dangerous and toxic. The tenants were advised to vacate so it could be demolished. Having nowhere else to go, they remained. Its fatal destiny came by fire a few years later.

Flames engulfed the old brewery in a forceful blaze. Sixteen families remained trapped inside among the orange glow of burning timbers. One lady awoke late to the discovery, with no way out save her window. She tossed her two children down from her second-story room into the arms of the men sent for rescue. Too afraid to jump, she waited until her clothes caught fire before braving the escape. She suffered severe burns to her legs and chest. Her ankle broke from the jump.

The Old Indianapolis Brewery burned to the ground; the fire had originated in the adjoining hay bailing shed. It was the last remaining relic of the city's first breweries—the end of the beginning. A new era was on the horizon.

THE GOLDEN ERA, 1890-1918

THE BIG THREE

Mr. and Mrs. Schmidt, 1859–1889

A cool, salty breeze caressed the loose ends of Caroline Schmidt's brunette locks as she sailed west across the Atlantic. A vast stretch of blue nothingness lay before her, a gray morning fog erasing the line between the ocean and the sky. Waves lapped at the hull of the ship.

It had been nearly a year since her brother, William Fieber, passed away, and just over three years since her husband died, leaving her with the brewery. She sailed in April 1875 to Germany with her family, leaving two of her three sons there to attend school. Traveling back to Indianapolis, she knew that she had a large business to attend to—the legacy of her late husband, Christian Frederick Schmidt.

In 1849, C.F. Schmidt immigrated to the United States from Germany. He was born in the city of Birkenfeld, Saxony, on November 23, 1830. There he received a good education. Mr. and Mrs. Schmidt married while living in Cincinnati, Ohio. The couple moved to Indianapolis in 1858. One year later, he established a brewery with his business partner, Charles Jaeger.

What these two entrepreneurial spirits lacked in monetary resources, they made up for with their youthful, optimistic energy. Together, they pooled what little money they had—$250 afforded them two lots of land on East

McCarty Street and South Alabama, on the corner of then High and Wyoming Streets. They roughed together a brewhouse and began brewing lagers. The brewery was two stories high, ninety-three by forty feet. There was also a two-and-a-half-story brick icehouse sixty by eighty feet, with cellars ninety-four by eighty-five feet.

After a few years, annual sales reached about 1,500 barrels. The progressive and ambitious Schmidt pushed for expansion, something that Jaeger would not support. He was of the opinion that Schmidt's ideas were too risky and would ruin the business. They were never able to reach an agreement. Jaeger sold his shares to Schmidt, and the partnership dissolved. In 1863, Jaeger established City Brewery on south Pennsylvania Street.

Schmidt moved forward with his expansion project. He invested $20,000 in a new brewery cellar. He also invested in town lots near his brewery, in the up-and-coming southernmost part of the city. The young neighborhood grew rapidly, proving an excellent return. Today, this area is known as Indy's Old Southside. The additional capital, along with a superior product and the dedication of his wife and sons throughout the years, helped the brewery grow into one of the best and largest in the West and the largest in Indianapolis. It was even one of the first commercial buildings in the city to get electricity.

The premises grew until it filled the whole block. It was so big that they called it "Schmidt's Square." It included the original brewery with its brick icehouse and cellars, as well as a new brick icehouse on the second story with a capacity for 1,800 tons of ice. More cellars were constructed of stone and iron, two stories in depth. There was a large stable and a two-story bottling house 60 by 130 feet. A new 40-by-115-foot addition served as a malt house and various other departments.

C.F. Schmidt became famous for his lagers. He also served as a city councilman for four years on the Republican ticket and was a member of the financial committee. According to *Pictorial & Biographical Memoirs*, during his term he "aided materially in rescuing the credit of the city, the paper of which then rated at a ruinous discount." He was also a member and director of the Guttenberg Printing and Publishing Company.

Christian Frederick Schmidt. *From* Nowland's Sketches of Prominent Citizens.

Schmidt's Brew House. *Indiana State Library.*

Schmidt passed away on February 3, 1872. "In all his business relations he was an honest, upright man, of large capabilities, extraordinary energy and progressive spirit. In his social relations as a citizen, as a neighbor and as the head of a family, he was alike respected, esteemed and loved. He was a generous aider of religious and charitable organizations and gave freely to the poor and destitute who came within his notice," according to *Pictorial & Biographical Memoirs.* At the time of his death, Schmidt's funeral was one of the largest ever witnessed in the city. In his last will and testament, he bequeathed all of his property to his widow, Caroline, and, after her, his sons.

MRS. SCHMIDT STOOD NEAR the ship's bow, looking out into the endless, distant blue. She thought of her late husband's brewery. Her brother had helped her manage the business after Mr. Schmidt passed. But now, upon his death, she carried sole responsibility.

It was rare for a woman in those days to work in the commercial brewing industry. It was especially unheard of for a woman to own a brewery or manage such an endeavor. Upon Mr. Schmidt's death, a local newspaper announced that his will advised the sale of the brewery. Mrs. Schmidt had other ideas. She pulled herself up by the bootstraps, pinned back her hair and rolled up her sleeves.

Even though they were in the midst of a financial panic, for Caroline, it was onward and upward. In 1875, she installed new vaults and cellars to accommodate a growing production. These improvements totaled a cost of about $20,000 (equivalent to nearly $500,000 today). The two cellars were each twenty feet deep, seventy-five feet long and thirty feet wide. At the time, they were acclaimed as being among the finest in the West. Shortly after, she purchased property on Shelby Street with Henry Metzger and Louis Ehrmann, dealers in groceries and provisions, on which to build a large brewery.

Six months after the announcement of this larger brewery, Henry Baas, a brewer and foreman at Schmidt's Brewery, left to form a partnership with Peter Balz to manage Union Brewery. Balz's business partner, Conrad Sponsel, died a few years earlier. In 1877, Balz changed the company name to Balz & Baas. It closed in 1879.

Mrs. Schmidt continued without Baas. No information exists regarding a brewery on Shelby. The next year, she commenced plans for an addition to the brewery on McCarty. It cost today's equivalent of more than $3 million. In *Nowland's Early Sketches*, to give an idea of the immense amount of business she managed, he stated that she paid out about $12,000 in ice alone (more than $250,000). In 1877, she produced more than twenty-two thousand barrels of beer, employed forty hands and a dozen teams for delivery.

Mrs. Schmidt was in the prime of her life at about forty years of age. Although she was very wealthy, Nowland described her as "unostentatious and prepossessing in her manners, and seems devoted to her business and the interest of her children." In spite of her good health, Caroline Schmidt became very ill for several weeks. She passed away in 1877, leaving behind an estate worth today's equivalent of more than $13 million.

When her sons John and Edward inherited the brewery upon her death, they continued with improvements. In 1878, they connected the cellars via an underground tunnel. In 1880, the largest iron columns ever made in the city were created for Schmidt's Brewery. Crowds would gather at the foundry to watch the columns being cast. Each weighed about seven thousand pounds and were cast at a rate of two per week. In 1881, the brewery expanded yet again when it added a bottling plant. In 1884, it added a $40,000 addition, likely a large icehouse, and later an ice manufacturing machine in 1887 at the cost of more than $25,000. In 1885, it gained approval to build a tramway over Wyoming Street. As far as transporting product, a local paper stated, "People don't agree as to the product of the concern, but there was no dissent from the opinion that Schmidt's brewery ten horse team is unequaled in these parts."

Brewery sales grew from 25,288 barrels of beer in 1879 to nearly 60,000 barrels in 1882. For a time, Schmidt's led the city with the largest output in beer production with a 100,000-barrel capacity per year. It had several agencies and distributed throughout Indiana and into Illinois. Eventually, it would merge with two other breweries and become world renowned. It seems that $250 in start-up capital was well worth the investment.

Pictorial & Biographical Memoirs describes John W. Schmidt as a self-made man: "Generally age and experience are essential to success and promotion. Prominent men seldom rise to distinction suddenly. But in the example before us, we have a man without any special fortuitous circumstances, rising by his own force of character, great energy and good judgment to the front ranks as a businessman." However, I imagine John would have attributed much of his success to his mother, who worked tirelessly to ensure that her sons had every opportunity to succeed. He was about twenty-one years of age when his mother passed and left him the brewery.

Schmidt's Tunnels. *Bass Photo Co. Collection, Indiana Historical Society, P0411.*

Above: Lower floor of Schmidt's brewhouse. *Indiana State Library.*

Left: Beer cellar at Schmidt's brewery. *Indiana State Library.*

Brewing equipment at Schmidt's brewery. *Indiana State Library.*

Labeling machines at Schmidt's plant. *Indiana State Library.*

John W. Schmidt, the eldest son, was born in Cincinnati in 1856 and subsequently came to Indianapolis with his parents. He attended public school and later an academy at Hoboken, New Jersey. When he returned home, he worked as a clerk at Citizen's National Bank for a year. Then he traveled and explored the country for eighteen months. Once he had his fill, he came home and entered into the brewing business. He married in 1885, settling down with Miss Lily Schude, whom his mother had adopted from Louisville, Kentucky, at the age of six.

Edward was three years younger than John. He followed a similar path of education, except after the academy in New Jersey, he attended college in Leipsic, Germany. He became associated for a time with the brewery, was a free-spirited youth, carved his own identity and traveled the world.

Peter Lieber and Company, 1864–1889

A bank failure in St. Paul prompted a young Peter Lieber to leave his Minnesota home in New Ulm—a colony he'd helped found with a sturdy group of fellow Germans. Lieber hailed from Düsseldorf, Germany. Born in May 1834, he received a high degree of education and learned the brush-making trade from his father. At about eighteen years of age, he left his boyhood home to make his own way in America. He settled in Cincinnati, Ohio, and took a position as foreman at a brush factory, where he managed about three hundred employees. He later moved to Minnesota with a group from Cincinnati's Social Turnverein, where they established New Ulm. There, he opened a general store and traded fur with the natives. He also helped develop a farm. His business became prosperous, and he amassed a good amount of wealth. He met his wife there and married Miss Sophia de St. Andre in 1860. She was born in Germany and of French lineage.

Shortly after, he enlisted to serve as a private in the Civil War for the Union. Sophie, in the meantime, went to stay with Peter's brother, Herman, at his home in Indianapolis. Lieber served for two years in the war until he was wounded and honorably discharged. He became known as the limping war veteran, walking with a limp until the end of his days.

When he returned home to New Ulm, a bank failure left him penniless, as noted in *Dunn's History*: "[H]e was practically compelled to make an entirely new start, but his inherent courage and ambition were equal to the facing of all emergencies encountered at this time, as ever afterward in his career."

Given that Lieber's wife and brother were living in the booming city of Indianapolis, he decided to make it their permanent home. Soon he became private secretary to Governor Oliver P. Morton of Indiana and served at his side until the end of the war. Morton was a distinguishable war governor, and the two remained friends.

In 1864, Lieber and business partner, Rudolph Gagg, formed Gagg & Company. The company later changed to Lieber & Company. It acquired City Brewery from Schmidt's former partner, Charles Jaeger, and owed possibly to his death, with financial backing from Lieber's brother, Herman, and Charles F. Mayer. Herman was Indy's first professional art dealer and established a successful art store. He seems to have had a business relationship with Gagg, who was later listed as an art dealer in Terre Haute. Mayer was a wealthy merchant who owned a grocery and general store.

Lieber knew nothing about brewing but employed the skill of a brewmaster named Geiger, while he focused on sales. The business grew rapidly from the start. Mayer retired in the 1870s and sold his interest to Peter. Herman sold his shares around 1880. By then, the brewery had become large enough to form a stock company called the P. Lieber Brewing Company. Lieber served as president and CEO.

In 1871, expansion projects enlarged brewing capacity. Lieber built another brewery down the road on Madison Avenue near Union Brewery. He also planned a cellar expansion at the original brewery on South Pennsylvania but abandoned the project during the financial Panic of 1873. Instead, he sold the brewery to a lumber company the following year. It demolished the brewery to make room for a large cabinet factory. Lieber continued at the new site in Madison near the Jeffersonville railroad. In 1878, he erected a $35,000 addition to the brewery, extending his reach on Madison Avenue by one hundred feet. It was comparable in size and popularity to that of Schmidt's Brewery, as noted in Nowland's *Sketches of Prominent Citizens*:

> *To say that his establishment, in size, is second to none in the city, except that of C.F. Schmidt's, and his articles inferior to none, is but doing simple justice. Mr. Lieber enjoys, to a high degree, the confidence and esteem of all classes of citizens....His is a fair illustration of what perseverance and industry, coupled with strict integrity and punctuality will accomplish in business. It is to such men as Mr. Lieber that this city is largely indebted for her present prosperity. While he is a good business man he is yet liberal, especially for charitable and benevolent purposes.*

Right: Peter Lieber. *From* Dunn's History of Greater Indianapolis.

Below: P. Lieber Brewing Company. This is possibly the original brewery on Pennsylvania Street. *From* Hyman's Handbook.

P. LIEBER BREWING COMPANY, 504 to 520 Madison Avenue, Indianapolis, Ind., U. S. A

Sketch of P. Lieber Brewing Company, circa 1880. *Indiana Album, the Joan Hostetler Collection.*

Mr. Lieber became heavily involved in the community. Politically, he was Republican until he became angered by the Prohibition plank and switched permanently to the Democratic Party in 1880. There was a proposal to amend the Constitution to prohibit the sale and manufacture of alcohol in Indiana. It passed the session of the legislator. The *Indiana State Sentinel* interviewed Mr. Lieber regarding the legislation. Maintaining his business-like composure, he stated for the newspaper:

> *Of course…this is fanaticism. An interference with individual liberty to which no people in any form of Government ever have submitted or ever will submit; but additional investments until the question is permanently settled would be impudent. I had determined to invest $40,000 in brick and mortar this year, but, under the circumstances, must decline. Now look at that. [The Schmidts] are already building largely, giving good employment to stone-cutters and masons and laborers. I suppose this will stop and all these men will be thrown out of employment….This is a side of the question that the temperance people never seemed to have examined.*

Lieber continued, breaking down the economic scope and impact of the liquor and brewing industry, rattling off numbers and statistics like a man who studied them daily:

> *The State of Indiana, last year* [1880] *manufactured 198,341 barrels of beer and paid a tax of $183,465.…Does any man believe that this revenue could have been raised by a direct tax?…Prohibition is not only fatal to our theory of government, but time has abundantly demonstrated its impracticability. There are some things that no legislative enactment can reach, and this thing of eating and drinking is one of them.*

He also argued that as the consumption of beer (which tended to be lower in alcohol) increased, the consumption of hard liquors decreased. From 1879 to 1880, there was an increase in beer production by 800,000 barrels in Indiana. He was of the opinion that beer would solve the temperance question in America.

In 1884, Lieber was a delegate to the National Democratic Convention. As he neared an age of retirement, his health began to decline. He retired to his homeland in 1888, living in a castle along the Rhine River. In his pride for America, he "hoisted the Stars and Stripes over his castle and lived his remaining days in opulence and official grandeur," according to *The Vonnegut Encyclopedia*.

Lieber had made a name for himself and was so highly esteemed that in 1893, President Cleveland appointed him consul to Düsseldorf. He served in that position until the office was abolished in 1908. During his time, he "made an admirable record as a representative of the interests of the United States," as noted in *Dunn's History*. He always kept in close touch with home in the States and his door always open to American tourists, particularly those from Indianapolis.

Peter Lieber was a man of great influence and left his mark on Indianapolis. *Pictorial and Biographical Memoirs of Indianapolis* recounts Lieber in the highest esteem:

> *This gentleman is regarded as one of the most influential and worthy citizens of Marion County, and it is a pleasure to chronicle here the events that mark his life as one of usefulness. Material wealth must not exclude the riches of character and ability in recounting the virtues which have been brought to this country by its citizens, and among its most precious treasurer must be estimated the lives of those citizens who have by their*

intelligence and their eminence in the higher walks of life, assisted in raising the standard of life and thought in the communities in which they have settled. No one has probably done more in this line than Peter Lieber.

Once Lieber resigned, his son Albert Lieber took over the business. He was about twenty-five years of age. Albert had attended the Indianapolis Business College and, before then, received the advantages offered by the German American schools, as well as private tutors. Upon graduating, he worked alongside his father at the brewery. He began first as an office boy and then bookkeeper. When the firm changed to P. Lieber Brewing Company, he was made treasurer. By the time Peter retired, Albert was well prepared to take his place.

Albert Lieber carried the brewery's legacy with indistinguishable success and, like his father, contributed greatly to the city. He showed "distinctive interest in the upbuilding of the larger and greater industrial city… attained prestige as one of the substantial and influential businessmen of his native city, where he has ever enjoyed the most unequivocal popular confidence and esteem," according to *Dunn's History*.

Casper Maus & Company, 1865–1889

Smoke billowed from the stable doors as Casper Maus rushed to free the horses from the engulfing flames. Time seemed to move both fast and slow with each panicked breath. Sweat poured from his face as he watched his beloved flour mill and stables turn to ash. The only remaining evidence was the smell of burned toast.

The year was 1863. Maus was commissioned as an enrolling officer during the Civil War for the Union. The Confederate Knights of the Golden Circle, radically opposed to drafting soldiers for the Union army, instigated the hate crime directed at Maus by burning down his business. He lost everything in the fire. It wasn't until many years later that the crime was confirmed when one of the party members, on his deathbed, confessed to the incendiary event. They may have destroyed Maus's business, but they could not destroy his spirit.

Casper Maus was a miller by trade and came from a prestigious family of millers dating back to the 1500s. Passed down through generations, the family mill was located in Eberbach, in his native land of Lorraine, France. Maus gave it up in 1835 for the dream of America. He arrived first to New Orleans, where he stayed for two years, and then moved to Cincinnati, where he continued in the milling business and manufacture of flour. During that time, he met his wife, Miss Magdalena M. Dietrich, who was also from France. The two married in 1842. They later moved to Indiana and settled at New Alsace in Dearborn County. There he erected the first steam gristmill in the eastern part of the state. He continued a successful milling business for about seventeen years until the Knights of the Golden Circle burned it to the ground, as Nowland noted in *Early Reminiscences*: "When he left his native home he thought he was coming to the 'land of the free and

Casper Maus. *From* Dunn's History of Greater Indianapolis.

the home of the brave,' but his experience in Dearborn county was a severe lesson to the contrary, but it is to be hoped that such a state of things will never again occur in our government."

Devastated, Maus moved his family to Indianapolis and started anew. They arrived in 1864. The following year, he began brewing with George Kalb and his eldest son, Albert Maus. Together they formed Casper Maus & Company. The brewery was located on the block between Alabama and Delaware, Washington and Maryland. In 1867, the company split. Maus continued brewing ale at a new location.

Many sources remember Maus's second brewery location on West New York and Agnes (now University Boulevard) Streets, at the current Indiana University–Purdue University at Indianapolis (IUPUI) campus. It was at this location where he saw the most success. The former miller also established Maus' Malt House and Kiln on the southwest corner of South and Delaware Streets.

In the early days, the C. Maus Brewery was famous for its bock beer. In addition, Maus represented the only brewery in town that could lay claim to being the purest. An ad in the newspaper boasted, "Scientific analysis has demonstrated that Maus Lager Beer is superior to all others, either as an exhilarating beverage or as a tonic for invalids." Another scientific analysis was taken at different seasons to show the consistency of the product. The result indicated that "the high percentage of Extract and Maltose [unfermented sugar] and the low percentage of Alcohol indicate that the BEER is a nutritious

C. Maus Brewery. *The Millers of Greenfield, Indiana.*

and wholesome beverage." Furthermore, "from the rather high percentage of Albuminoids, Lactic Acid and Ash, we would judge that the Beer is a PURE MALT BEER, no substitute for malt having been used."

C. Habich & Company, founded by Carl Habich Sr., a pioneer of Indianapolis, purchased the exclusive right to bottle Maus's Lager and Tafel beer. A certificate, which claimed the beer's purity of only malts and hops as ingredients in its manufacture, was on every bottle.

Casper Maus maintained a successful brewing business until his death in January 1876 following a painful illness. In *Sketches of Prominent Citizens*, Nowland wrote of Maus, "During his residence in Indianapolis, he made many warm and valued friends, who will long remember his kind and generous disposition, his polite and gentlemanly bearing."

According to *Dunn's History*, he was "a man of inflexible integrity and honor in all the relations of life and ever evinced the utmost loyalty to the land of his adoption…a man of much business acumen and of indefatigable energy, and he attained to a large measure of success through his own well directed efforts after coming as a stranger to a strange land. He was generous and hospitable, tolerant and kindly in his relations with his fellow men, and he left the heritage of a good name."

Maus left behind a wife, five sons and two daughters. His widow, Magdalena, inherited ownership of the brewery. His third son, Frank A. Maus, had graduated from a local commercial college in 1867 and associated himself with the business. At about twenty-five years of age, after his father's death, Frank became general manager for the benefit of the family. He continued with the brewery's success.

Casper's other sons had involvement in the brewery as well. Albert kept the books and also brewed. Matthias had been a brewer and continued as a foreman. Casper Jr. later signed on to help with bookkeeping.

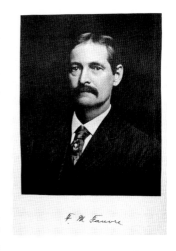

Frank Maus Fauvre. *From* Dunn's History of Greater Indianapolis.

A few years after his father's death, Frank Maus made plans to expand the brewery. He began a $10,000 addition in 1879. In 1881, he installed the city's first artificial ice plant. He continued with additions and extensive improvements in the following years. By 1887, he had completed improvements, which included new boilers, a new engine and two seventy-five-horsepower boilers. In 1889, an extensive addition to his plant at West New York Street was considered one of the finest buildings in the city.

Frank was a progressive, forward-thinking businessman, loyal to his community and heavily vested in its betterment. He was even elected to the city council. While he maintained a successful brewing business, he was most prominently known for his work in ice manufacturing. He established several large and modern artificial ice plants in Indianapolis and other cities. He also had business in coal mining operations throughout Indiana and took interest in the promotion of public utilities. He became associated with the purchase of an electric interurban line extending between Indianapolis and Greenfield in 1902, for which he was a stockholder, executive officer and later president. The line was improved and extended under his leadership. It was one of the most important interurban systems in the city. He also owned a mortgage on a zoo located at North Mississippi Street. The zoo also served as a variety theater and drinking resort.

As a funny side note, in 1900, Frank Maus changed his name to Frank M. Fauvre, the name of his paternal grandmother. The local newspaper stated that he wished for the name change because he was tired of people referring to him as "Mr. Mouse" when the correct pronunciation was closer to "moss." His children also adopted the new surname. Frank retired from brewing around this time, and the brewery converted into a storage and malt house until it sold in 1902.

A LIT MATCH TO LEAD THE WAY

The match slid, popped and sizzled in the dark night of Eaton, Indiana. A group of citizens gathered in anticipation to watch the lighting stick cautiously make its way to an upward gust of gas springing forth from the earth. Suddenly, like a magician's act, a great *whoosh* revealed a magnificent ten-foot-tall fiery beacon of light. Everyone cheered as they stepped back to revel in the glory of the giant flickering torch—a symbol of hope and prosperity.

Indiana experienced a natural gas boom in the 1880s and 1890s. It's regarded as one of the most dramatic eras in the state's history and one of the great natural resource discoveries of American history. It catapulted Indiana from an agricultural state into an industrial behemoth. It's been compared to and fashioned as a type of gold rush for Indiana. Mighty torches burned day and night to show off the abundance of gas, acting as a billboard to attract investors.

The first commercial well to produce a profitable supply was located in Eaton, a town near Muncie. In the excitement, drilling quickly spread across east-central Indiana. Indianapolis soon joined the gas craze and built pipelines to tap into the supply. Investors included owners of the city's largest breweries: Frank Maus, brothers John and Edward Schmidt and Peter Lieber. Indy latched on to the gas boom and benefited from the development of new markets in the boomtowns of the region. As a result, the city experienced yet another wave of rapid growth as it captivated an immeasurable amount of new wealth.

As the economy erupted, so did improvements to technology and transportation. The Industrial Revolution, which had begun in Great Britain, made its way to the United States and eventually Indianapolis. This turning point in history changed the world and influenced nearly every aspect of daily life, including beer.

Scientific and technological developments changed the way beer was produced and consumed. Pasteurization helped extend shelf life. Inventions like the roasting drum, black patent malt and hydrometers allowed more

Indiana gas well, 1887. *Indiana Album, the Joan Hostetler Collection.*

consistency and control over the final product. Artificial refrigeration (invented specifically for brewing) expanded the availability of cold-fermented lagers. Steam engines, modern factories, improved railways and refrigerated railcars fostered greater beer production. Demand increased as the population grew and the working class received higher wages.

Beer production went from hand-crafted to machine-made, from domestic and town artisanal breweries to mass-producing beer factories, from rugged farmhouse ales to clean, shelf-stable lagers and from community taverns along dirt roads to giant banners in the city square advertising the world's finest, as noted in *Dunn's History*:

> *What was then determined by instinct, has come to be an exact science. The old-time brewmaster who "guessed by practice," has given place to the modern brewmaster, the skilled chemist, who not only brings to his aid years of practice, but has the many advantages that ingenuity has brought with the use of modern appliances. Thus, the beer of today, is the combined result of years of practical experience and chemical skill. How well the public have appreciated the efforts of those engaged in the manufacture of this popular beverage to bring it to its very highest standard of excellence and purity, is evidenced in the many millions invested in great plants all over the country and the annually growing consumption.*

Beer in Indianapolis had waited a long time for its big moment in the spotlight. Indy's rugged beginnings, with its start in isolation due to lack of roads and navigable waterways, followed by temperance and xenophobic movements and financial panics, had flushed out many of the city's early breweries.

A lot had changed since the days of Nowland's tavern and scattered log cabins nestled in a dense forest of hardwood trees. Indianapolis had become one of the most important manufacturing and commercial centers of the country—a bustling, vibrant, energetic city of wholesale trade and industry. The synergy of the railways transformed the once small town into a major transportation hub connected to a world of possibility. Union Station outgrew its original facility and moved into its new, current-standing Romanesque station in 1888. By then, Indy had well earned its status as the "Railway City."

Steam locomotives embarking Union Station whistled loudly their presence as they chugged through city blocks. Smoke rose with the scent of burning coal along the track through stories-tall brick buildings and

Indianapolis Wholesale District. *Bass Photo Co. Collection, Indiana Historical Society.*

arcading Italianate façades, painted on the sides with advertisements for local provisions. The breweries that had weathered the storms opened up the floodgates to the flowing goodness of beer.

Notes of floral, mint and spice swirled in the air as the machine at Schmidt's Brewery tore apart hops in preparation for brewing. They'd arrived in four-hundred-pound sacks—the finest imported from Germany. Malted cereal grains dropped 550 bushels at a time into a giant mash tub filled with the purest of hot water. They soaked three hours until the grainy liquid was drained from its porridgey bath into a brilliantly polished copper kettle.

Schmidt's acclaimed copper kettle was one of the most impressive in the West. It hung between two floors and was shaped like a giant pear. Modern for its time, it operated with steam instead of a fire to heat it from beneath.

Next, three hundred pounds of hops were added and left to boil for five hours. Then the remnants were separated from the liquid. The soon-to-be beer continued on its journey. It traveled about a half mile through meticulously cleaned copper pipes. It was pumped upstairs and circulated through a series of horizontal pipes for cooling and then downstairs into fermenting vats, where yeast had been "washed, analyzed and freed from all harmful bacteria," as was described. This initial process took sixteen hours. The liquid left to ferment for about three weeks. It would then be cellared in casks that stood two stories high, where it would "rest."

Schmidt's famous cellars lay fifty feet underground and covered several acres—an endless maze of vaults connected by tunnels. It was like a dungeon of an old chateau. There were eleven cellars. Some contained casks as large as a small house, capable of holding 2,750 gallons each.

An employee acting as tour guide leaned against a massive stone pillar of the subterranean cavern. The sound produced by the *thump* of his fist against one of the casks demonstrated that it was full of beer. The light from his lantern flickered beneath the stone arches, outlining the giant vats in a ghostly manner. His breath was traceable in the dim light. "If I should leave you down here you would freeze to death before you could find your way out," mentioned the tour guide during a July tour in 1885, as the guests inspected the coating of ice and frost on the iron pipes that ran across the ceiling. The cellar's cooling rooms maintained its freezing temperature through use of a state-of-the-art ammonia refrigeration system. "After the beer has a chance to rest," continued the guide, "it travels even further down into the cellar and placed in great chip casks where it'll be bunged up and left to rest on its side. Here, the beer becomes naturally carbonated during four weeks' time. The entire process, from start to finish, takes about six months."

It was the very beginning of Indianapolis's golden era of brewing, led by the "Big Three": Schmidt, Lieber and Maus. It was through the ambition and drive of generations that these three breweries proved their capabilities and longevity through challenging times. In 1889, they would combine forces into the legendary and world-renowned Indianapolis Brewing Company. As Hyman noted:

> *Tracing the history of this institution backward, we find it contemporaneous with that period which has marked the city's development from a rough western village to a magnificent metropolis, second to no other city, in the character and solidity of its growth. Side by side with its development, beginning in the humblest and most unpretentious manner, this business has grown until today it has expanded to such proportions as to be classed*

among the ten of the largest enterprises in America. When it is remembered that there are but two other lines of industries in the country aggregating a greater amount of invested capital, it becomes a matter of justifiable pride to refer to it in this connection.

Other breweries soon followed suit. The Home Brewing Company established itself in 1891, followed by the American Brewing Company in 1897 and Capital City Brewing in 1905. Even major outside breweries saw benefit to setting up shop in Indianapolis. Schlitz, Blatz, Anheuser-Busch and Pabst established bottling and distribution agencies along with saloons in the city, as well as the Terre Haute and Crescent Breweries of Indiana. Crescent Brewing's depot was located next to Maus' Malt House and Kiln.

Joseph Charles Schaf came to Indianapolis from Cincinnati in 1887. His family maintained connections with the Maus family. Schaf's grandparents also hailed from Lorraine, France (which later became a German province), and settled in Dearborn County after coming to America in 1838. In 1887, Schaf married Frank Maus's daughter, Miss Josephine Maus. Shortly after, he began work at Maus's brewery under the title of assistant manager. Ten years later, he established the American Brewing Company with help from his father-in-law. It appears that around this time Maus discontinued at his brewing plant and became associated instead with the American Brewing Company.

Schaf is credited as the first native-born American to establish a brewery in Indianapolis. It was founded with $130,000 in capital stock. He purchased an ice company for $40,000 and built an addition for $8,376. The brewery was located on the corner of Ohio and Missouri Streets near the canal. Schaf served as president, Anthony J. Krass was vice-president and Herman Habich was secretary. They produced about thirty thousand barrels per year and had twenty-eight employees. They were most noted for their German weiss beer and Bohemian lager. Schaf also served as secretary and treasurer of C. Habich & Company, along with Frank Maus, who served as vice-president. Likely, the Habich Company bottled the American Brewing Company's products as it had also been bottling Maus's brewery's beer.

Starting in 1911, the American Brewing Company sponsored the Indianapolis ABCs, an independent professional baseball team in the Negro Leagues. Charles I. Taylor managed and co-owned the Indianapolis ABCs starting in 1914. Prior to his time with the Indianapolis team, he founded the first Black professional baseball team, the Birmingham Giants. Later, in

This page, top: American Brewing Company (behind Paul Krauss Laundry), 1910. *Bass Photo Co. Collection, Indiana Historical Society.*

This page, bottom: Tied house, American Brewing Company (cropped from original image). *Bass Photo Co. Collection, Indiana Historical Society.*

Opposite: American and Home Brewing Company bottles and serving tray. *Dave Worthington Collection.*

1920, he cofounded and served as vice-president of the first Negro National League, to which the ABCs became a charter member.

Taylor created a legacy as a pioneer in professional baseball. He developed the Indianapolis ABCs into a powerhouse team, a force matched only by their rival, Rube Foster's Chicago American Giants. In 1916, Taylor led the team to the western championship of Black baseball. This win against the Giants established the ABCs as one of the great pre–Negro National League teams ever fielded. It was the pinnacle of Taylor's managerial career.

In an article for the Society for American Baseball, Bill Johnson wrote, "After the on-field successes, the executive brilliance, the leadership in supporting Foster's bid to organize the NNL, and his demeanor and character as a human being, he greatly affected the future of the game."

Taylor lived at 440 Indiana Avenue in Indianapolis, a neighborhood where he also maintained a pool hall. During the off-season, he employed several of his players at the pool hall, where he likely served the American Brewing Company's beer. According to *Hoosier Beer*, he also owned an interest in the brewing company.

Then there were the outside breweries. Anheuser-Busch, one of the largest and most prominent breweries in the country, had a brewing capacity of 1.8 million barrels annually. It established an Indianapolis agency in 1891. Beer

Anheuser-Busch Brewing Association Building, Indianapolis, 1911. The wagon features Budweiser Beer. *Bass Photo Co. Collection, Indiana Historical Society.*

was transported from the main brewery in St. Louis to Indianapolis. From there, it would be stored, bottled and distributed. It was located at East and Ohio Streets on a three-acre plot. The bottling plant was two stories high, 40 by 160 feet in dimension and equipped with the best machinery. Its storage facility was equipped with the latest refrigeration technology and had a capacity for sixteen carloads of beer. There were twenty-five employees and six delivery wagons. It was managed by a Mr. J.L. Bieler, who emigrated from Germany and came to Indianapolis in 1861.

The Terre Haute Brewery was established in Indiana in 1837. By the turn of the century, it had become the seventh largest in the country. It established a plant in Indianapolis, the same year as Anheuser-Busch. It was located at South and West Streets near current Victory Field. In its first year, this branch sold 8,000 barrels of beer. The second year, sales rose to 11,000 barrels. Around 1897, sales reached a total of 26,000 barrels. The company in its entirety had an annual output of about 100,000 barrels of beer. It became most famous for Champagne Velvet, a lager now brewed by Upland Brewing Company of Indiana.

Crawford Fairbanks led the brewing company as president, and Edward P. Fairbanks was general manager. The local Indianapolis branch was managed by Maurice Donnelly. C. Habich & Company also bottled Terre Haute's products and made its own mineral water. C. Fairbanks served as the bottling company's director, alongside officers Schaf and Maus. It bottled three thousand barrels of beer annually.

As the brewing industry reached new heights, some saloonkeepers grew tired of the monopoly breweries had with their tied houses. In 1904, more than one hundred of these saloonkeepers pooled together $250,000 in capital to form Capital City Brewing. They incorporated on August 6, broke ground in November and laid the cornerstone the following year in April 1905. The new, modern brewing plant was located on five acres at West and Morris Streets near a railway. They acquired the site from President Theodore Roosevelt, who'd inherited the land as part of an estate—a butter dish factory once existed there. They built the first story with Indiana limestone and the upper stories in red brick, with pressed brick front and stone trimmings. They planned the capacity for output at seventy-five thousand barrels per year—much larger than most of the other breweries. These saloonkeepers must have been awfully confident in their start-up business. By 1906, they'd reached over three hundred stockholders.

Charles Krauss was president, John J. Giesen vice-president and Victor R. Jose secretary and treasurer. Giesen was brewmaster at the Indianapolis Brewing Company until he quit to help form Capital City

Terre Haute Brewing Company, Indianapolis Branch. *From* Hyman's Handbook.

Above: Capital City Brewing, 1906. *Bass Photo Co. Collection, Indiana Historical Society.*

Opposite, top: Illustration of Capital City Brewing, 1911. *Bass Photo Co. Collection, Indiana Historical Society.*

Opposite, bottom: Capital City Brewing Company's Taste Tells bottles. *Dave Worthington Collection (left); the Millers of Greenfield, Indiana (right).*

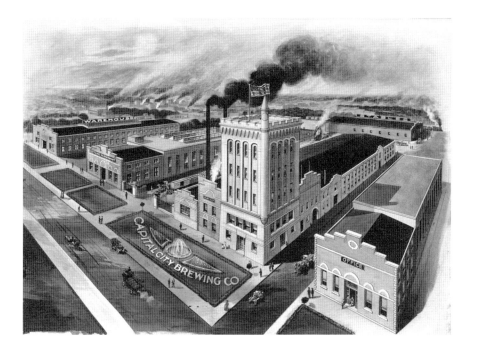

Brewing. Jose stated to the *Indianapolis Star* that "no fight will be made on other breweries, nor will the new company compete for outside trade at first," he insisted. "The intention is simply to manufacture beer for the independent saloons and return a dividend to the independent saloon keepers. However, the company will make a bid for trade of saloons other than the independent ones, as it will run a bottling department that will probably be put into operation at an early date." Its brands included Capital City Brew; T.T. ("Taste Tells"), a light beer; Frauenlob, a dark beer; and Camel's Milk.

The lit match began to burn hot as competition, and tempers among brewers, rose. Albert Lieber, of the Indianapolis Brewing Company, and Victor Jose became sworn enemies. Each claimed that the other resorted to tricks to try to put the other out of business. There were several assaults between the opposing employees where "blood flowed freely." A brewing war ensued. Each had their respective breweries guarded at night. The Indianapolis Brewing Company and Capital City Brewing intertwined in controversy and conspiracy theories as they went for each other's throats.

LEGACY OF THE INDIANAPOLIS BREWING COMPANY

Controversial rumors that had been simmering for the past year finally came to a roaring boil in October 1889. A reporter from the *Indianapolis Journal* went looking for John W. Schmidt that Tuesday afternoon. He was not at the brewery. He was not home. Nobody seemed to know his whereabouts. Upon a chance encounter, the reporter bumped into an employee of the brewery who tipped him off to his location.

The reporter swung open the door to a rowdy saloon near the brewery. He found Schmidt drinking at the bar, protected by a wall of men. He cut through the loud, chattering buzz, belting out to Schmidt, "Is it true?!" The clamoring saloon noise fell to a decrescendo of quiet whispers. Schmidt slowly turned to face the man.

"I cannot say," remarked Schmidt, waiting in anticipation, for he knew the next question.

"Will you deny the statement to the effect that you have sold the brewery to an English syndicate!" retorted the reporter without missing a beat.

"I have not seen such statement," Schmidt replied, giving a playful wink to one of his employees standing nearby. The reporter pressed him, but he would give no clear answer. Finally, Schmidt slammed his fist on the table, took a swig of British ale and in a defiant statement remarked, "You can't pump me!" With that, he ended the interview.

The reporter moved in search of Frank Maus, but he was nowhere to be found. He then discovered Albert Lieber, son of Peter Lieber, who had recently retired to Germany. Young Albert had just taken over the business. He was in his office when the reporter approached with his questions.

After some thought and hesitation, Lieber responded, "Of course. There has been a deal made. $2,500,000 will come to this city, and it will all be invested here."

Brewing in the United States became a major industry in the latter part of the nineteenth century. Meanwhile, the Industrial Revolution had catapulted Great Britain into a bustling economic power force. British capitalists began looking to foreign investment opportunities to grow their wealth.

British capital flowed into the United States in unprecedented amounts from 1888 to 1892. Although they turned to several different industries, the brewing industry was a primary target. They formed syndicates and selected only the choicest properties. This divided the American nation.

One side welcomed the British capital, believing it an opportunity to help feed a fledgling economy. Some also believed that it would solidify peaceful allies. On the other hand, given the history between the two, others feared that it would give the British too much control. There was concern of money leaking out of the country. Many thought that these breweries who "fell to English syndicates" were selling out. Some of the country's leading breweries, however, including Anheuser-Busch and Pabst, did not succumb to the syndicates.

As the American industry grew, so did competition. This period of new growth was also marked by limited capital for continued growth. British capital, and merging to reduce competition, was an answer.

Indianapolis's three major breweries—the Schmidt, Maus and Lieber Breweries—had been in spirited negotiations for the past twelve months. An English syndicate representative from Boston by the name of H.M. Bigelow arrived to the city's most elegant Grand Hotel. It was a Sunday evening. He was accompanied by two New York attorneys. The following Tuesday morning, on October 15, 1889, they held a conference at the hotel to seal the deal. Schmidt, Maus and Lieber Breweries merged to form the Indianapolis Brewing Company. It was officially incorporated on January 11, 1890.

In addressing public concern over wide-reaching British control, Lieber continued his comment to the reporter:

The only interest that will be taken in the working of the breweries by the English capitalists, will be that twice yearly accountants will be sent here to examine the books of the breweries….There is no such thing as a syndicate of English trying to monopolize the brewing interests of the United States. There is a "crowd," that is, a number of Englishmen who have a surplus of funds, and, wishing to invest in a good thing, have appointed agents in America to inform them of paying investments, but there is no regular organization. The Englishmen I represent have no connection with those who have purchased the breweries in Chicago, though one or two of them may have purchased some of the stock of the local parties. As for buying the controlling interest in the breweries, there is nothing in it.

Under the merger, Schmidt, Maus and Lieber owned majority controlling shares. Albert Lieber became president. Maus became vice-president and John Schmidt served on the board of directors for many years. Each maintained management and brand recognition of their respective breweries and operated as separate entities. Each was paid a handsome salary in addition to the $2.5 million received from the purchase. Schmidt and Lieber each received about $1 million, with the rest going to Maus. Needless to say, these brewery owners became quite wealthy almost overnight. The amount invested by the English syndicate would be the equivalent of more than $75 million today. As time passed, Schmidt and Maus tended to their shares but had less direct involvement with the brewery, turning to other interests. Albert Lieber became the main figure associated with the Indianapolis Brewing Company.

"I think it is one of the biggest deals ever effected here," continued Lieber to the reporter, "and the influence of such a large sum of money will give Indianapolis the boom which she needs." He continued, explaining that the money would be invested into property and other improvements for the city.

At the beginning of the merger, total output by the three breweries was expected to be 160 barrels of beer daily. Schmidt would produce 85 barrels, Maus 35 and Lieber 40, with plans for expansion and increased production. Lieber expounded on the details of the deal to the reporter: "No employee will be affected by the transaction. The money paid over will be invested here.…The quality of beer, which has always stood high, will be bettered as we shall be able to send our agents out to buy up a larger and more expensive quality of material, which before we could not afford to do."

The following year, money received from the syndicate bolstered demand for real estate in Indianapolis. The wealthy brewers purchased several properties and town lots for development. Most notable were as follows. Maus invested in several lots at Washington and Capital, where he erected a four-story business block. He also purchased the Franklin Building on Market and Circle streets for $40,000. He made improvements and leased the space for office use. At one point, it served as the Indianapolis Brewing Company's head office. The building has since been demolished and replaced by the Art Deco Circle Tower that currently houses a Starbucks.

The Schmidt brothers built the Century Building. It originally housed office space. It's located near the present-day Gainbridge Fieldhouse and currently houses the Tin Roof, O'Reilly's Irish Pub, Coaches Tavern and Pearl Street Pizza. Also, they purchased the block on Pennsylvania between Washington and Market where Big Red Liquors now stands and a building between Meridian and Illinois on the north side of Georgia Street where the Circle Center Mall currently resides.

John Schmidt also contracted the firm Nuerge & Reinking to build a large, eclectic-style mansion for his family at 1410 North Delaware Street in 1890–91. It included Neo-Jacobean, Romanesque and Georgian elements, with an overall appearance of Queen Anne style. At the time, it was considered the finest residence in Indiana. Located in Indy's Near Northside, this lavish neighborhood, nicknamed the "Gold Coast," was where Indy's high society lived. Big names like L.S. Ayres, famed author Meredith Nicholson and former president Benjamin Harrison lived just a few doors down. The Schmidts lived there for twelve years. In 1905, the home stayed within the brewing business when it was sold to Joseph C. Schaf, president of the American Brewing Company of Indianapolis. The building now serves as the Indianapolis Propylaeum, a place that connects and celebrates women. Also known as the old Schmidt-Schaf House, it is listed in the National Register of Historic Places.

John Schmidt's younger brother, Edward, opted for less involvement with the brewery. He took his money and traveled extensively. In 1893, he completed a trip around the world.

Lieber invested in many downtown city blocks and buildings as well. Lots included the southeast corner of Georgia and Meridian Streets, where Kilroy's Bar and Grill and Meridian Lofts now stand.

In total, an amount of $727,335, or what would be today's equivalent of $21,820,290, of the brewing syndicate money was invested into the city of Indianapolis that year, with plans to invest more. "The realty market has not been better for years than it is at the present time," stated an article in the *Indianapolis Journal*. "Local capitalists attribute the recent increase in investments to a steady growth rather than any sudden boom, and there is no indication whatever of this spirit of activity declining. The recent sale of the breweries to an English syndicate has resulted in the receipts being invested in city property."

Beer helped build the city. Together with the gas boom and increasing railroad traffic, foreign investments helped transform Indianapolis into a midwestern industrial center. It ushered the city into a golden era of brewing starting around 1890 and ending with Prohibition in 1918.

Under Albert Lieber's leadership, the Indianapolis Brewing Company became one of the largest breweries in the country. According to *Dunn's History*, it was one of the most important industrial enterprises of its kind in the state, the largest and best equipped in the city.

Around 1901, the brewing plant was improved with the installation of glass-enameled steel chip tanks. The old brewing methods employed the use of wooden tubs. These would often harbor bacteria that could lead to spoilage and sour-tasting beer. These glass-enameled steel tanks allowed more consistency, a cleaner-finishing product and less beer dumped down the drain.

Lieber also patented an air hoist for a bottling line. The invention let down a tray of twenty-nine dozen bottles simultaneously into a steam trap. It did the work of six men.

By law in those days, bottling had to be kept separate from the brewing operation. As the Indianapolis Brewing Company gained recognition, its bottling facility became especially famous. It used a new method: rather than drawing beer from the cask, it used compressed air from the brewery. Beer went directly from vats to the bottle, where it was hermetically sealed to prevent oxidation. It was referred to as a model by the First American Academy of Science in New York. It maintained absolute cleanliness, down to every detail. Thousands came every year to visit the new establishment. The IBC's reputation became so high that the sons of the most famous brewers across the nation visited the bottling house to learn the improved methods.

Hyman's Handbook, published in 1897, paints this picture of the Indianapolis Brewing Company's magnificence:

> *Regarding the product of the Indianapolis Brewing Company, its fame has become international, second to none, and from Maine to California, and from Canada to Cuba, is the demand for it increasing. The total output of the Company for 1895, was in excess of 200,000 barrels, and the total brewing capacity of the combined plants will aggregate over 600,000*

From left to right: Frank Maus, Albert Lieber and John Schmidt (likely). *The Millers of Greenfield, Indiana.*

barrels per annum. The united plants cover an immense space, and are models of perfect equipment, with their great storehouses, brew houses, offices, boiler houses, ice machines, and refrigerator houses, warehouses, malt houses, wash and bottling houses, elevators, stables, cooper shops, shipping and packing departments, etc.

When it is taken into consideration that it employs directly and indirectly about 1,200 men, with wages ranging from $60 per month up to the high salary brewmaster who receives $10,000 per annum [about $325,000 today], *and the vast sums of money that are annually spent in building and equipments, all of which go into local circulation, beside paying into the city treasury by far more taxes than any other institution, the benefits derived from it by the community can not be overestimated.*

The Indianapolis Brewing Company's portfolio of beer included Bock, Budweiser, Cream Ale, Dublin Porter, Wiener, Export, Stock Ale and Tonica brewed at the Schmidt plant. It also brewed Valentine Beer, which was a malt

Indianapolis Brewing Company wagon, circa 1942. *Indiana Album, the Elizabeth Laslie Collection.*

Marion Park Hotel, tied house of the Indianapolis Brewing Company (cropped from original image). *Indiana Historical Society, P0411.*

Top: Gold Medal Lager label, from the Indianapolis Brewing Company. *The Millers of Greenfield, Indiana.*

Bottom: Indianapolis Brewing Company advertisement for Duesseldorfer, circa 1900s. *The Millers of Greenfield, Indiana.*

extract. Maus' Brewery brands included Champagne, Hop Ale, Half and Half, Pale Ale, Olden English Ale and, later, Progress and Duesseldorfer. The Lieber brands included Special Brew, Olden Time Ale, Porter, Wurzburger Style, Hoosier Beer and, later, Tafel and Gold Medal Lager.

By the turn of the century, the Indianapolis Brewing Company had introduced a new Progress Brand series that included its most popular Gold Medal, Tafel and Duesseldorfer beers. *Tafel* is the German word for "table," to represent table beer. Duesseldorfer is a style that originated from Peter Lieber's hometown of Düsseldorf, Germany.

These "beers of progress" reflected the social, economic and political climate during the Gilded Age of rapid industrial expansion and the building of an American empire. Several Progress brand advertisements acted as a type of political cartoon, with many featuring a caricature of Uncle Sam. The Progress series was distributed all across the United States and exported to Hawaii, Canada, Mexico, Cuba, Puerto Rico, Argentina, other parts of Central and South America, Africa, China, Japan and the Philippines.

The Indianapolis Brewing Company began entering its beer into prestigious competitions. In 1900, it proved it was the best at the World's Fair in Paris. Judges from across the globe performed scientific tests for quality and purity. Labels had been scratched off so winners were made by merit alone. The fair handed out twenty awards: one gold medal, nine silver, eight bronze and two honorable mentions. The gold

Indianapolis Brewing Company Duesseldorfer tray. *The Millers of Greenfield, Indiana.*

medal went to the Indianapolis Brewing Company's Duesseldorfer lager. It was "the highest achievement in the art of brewing." Indianapolis celebrated the momentous occasion during a citywide parade.

Indianapolis welcomed the returning officers and representatives of the company from the Paris World's Fair in the Merchants' and Manufacturers' Parade, celebrating the industrial interests of the city. Massive wagons and decorated floats pulled by huge draft horses gathered along Washington Street. The *clip-clop* of hooves progressed down the brick road to the cadence of the marching band. Cheers of approval came like waves from the sea of adoring locals and out-of-town guests. The scene was a flurry of proud banners flapping in the air and showcases of the latest goods. There were giant sculptures on top of painted carts embellished with flowers and adorned in colorful decoration. Men in uniform and ladies dressed in thematic characters rode atop the wagons. Some walked whimsically alongside the floats, waving to the crowd of approving fans.

The Indianapolis Brewing Company led the manufacturers' division. Its team of two wagons marched just behind the band. The display took up a great deal of space, garnering much attention and enthusiasm wherever it went. Three knights on horses escorted the exhibit and attended to King Gambrinus, a European cultural icon of beer, brewing and joviality. This was closely followed by the IBC's handsome new automobile, decorated in carnival colors with a pleasing mixture of white. The experience reached

Above: Indianapolis Brewing Company Banner featuring Duesseldorfer Beer, circa 1900s. *The Millers of Greenfield, Indiana.*

Right: Indianapolis Brewing Company's Duesseldorfer bottle. *The Millers of Greenfield, Indiana.*

a crescendo with four horses drawing the first large float, which vividly displayed the "art of brewing." Six dwarfs attended the display on foot. Falstaff, another iconic beer-loving fictional character, sat in the front with his back leaning against a cask, with men on each side dressed in seventeenth-century attire. The back of the float contained kegs, a brewing kettle and a mash tub attended by maltsters. A team of six magnificent horses pulled the finale float, occupied by a young lady dressed as a goddess with golden wings and holding up a chalice of beer—representing the IBC's angelic trademark figure. Another young lady represented France, while a man dressed as Uncle Sam led the float and represented the awarding of the gold medal at the Paris Exposition. The crowd cheered wildly with applause.

Duesseldorfer also won grand prize gold at the St. Louis World's Fair in 1904. Competing against other brewing giants, out of 117 entries, the Indianapolis Brewing Company won the highest honor. "Indianapolis has knocked Milwaukee off her perch," stated the *Indy Star*. It also won gold medals at Belgium in 1905, Milan and Paris in 1906 and Madrid in 1907. It was the height of its existence. By 1907, the company was brewing more than 1 million barrels per year.

The Indianapolis Brewing Company continued winning awards throughout Europe and America. Over the course of eleven years, Duesseldorfer won more gold medals, grand prizes and crosses of honor than any other beer brand in the world, earning a reputation as the "world's standard of perfection." One advertisement boasted, "[T]he best beer ever brewed, anywhere at anytime." Famed author Kurt Vonnegut Jr., who was Albert Lieber's grandson, disclosed the key ingredient: Gold Medal Duesseldorfer's big secret was *coffee*.

Man with an Indianapolis Brewing Company delivery wagon, circa 1910. *Indiana Album.*

Men of the Indianapolis Brewing Company, circa 1909. *Indiana Album, the Joan Hostetler Collection.*

Duesseldorfer sign at the corner of Kentucky Avenue, Illinois and Washington Streets, 1913. *Indiana Historical Society, P0236.*

A HOME REBELLION

Irishman (to English capitalist)—"If you don't stop buying American breweries, we will boycott your stuff and ruin you!"

English Capitalist—"We dare you to do it! Then we will buy up your distilleries, too, and make you come down on your knees for a drink of whiskey!"

—humorously poked an 1889 Indianapolis newspaper

The capitalists surreptitiously descended on the city, careful to avoid reporters, with some giving false names. One lurked through the shadows. He slithered into a brewery, only to be met with a firm, "We have nothing to sell except beer." Agents of outside breweries met with Irish saloonkeepers, urging them to buy their beer because, "Soon, many of your local breweries will be owned by the English. Don't give your money to people who are not friends of the Irish."

Dissension and prejudice began to circulate. Huge amounts of foreign investment capital poured into the United States. British syndicates were buying up a bunch of breweries. Many feared that accepting money from the English meant giving up control and worried that it would lead to economic ruin. One businessman wrote to the *Indianapolis Journal*:

> *It is not so very long ago that the entire press of the country made a great outcry against foreigners holding large tracts of land in the West.…At present, foreign capital is largely engaged in buying some of our greatest industries. It is a rare thing to open a newspaper nowadays which does not contain the announcement that such and such factories, breweries, iron-works and gas plants have been sold to a syndicate; and the press welcomes these events and enthusiastically endorses this influx of British gold. Can you explain why foreigners should not own the broad acres of the West, when you bid them welcome to our greatest industries?…it does not require much foresight to predict the time when there will be only two classes of people in this free Republic—the capitalist and the hired servant.*

After the purchase of the Indianapolis Brewing Company by an English syndicate, many of Indy's saloonkeepers became hostile and refused to deal in its products. They began importing beer from St. Louis and Cincinnati breweries. Because of the tied-house business model, in which breweries leased saloons under exclusive terms, some worried that they would not receive the credit or financial aid to which they'd become accustomed. Fear of the unknown aroused a sense of anxiety and insecurity over the future.

In response to this growing concern, a group of local moneyed men met quietly to discuss investing largely in another Indianapolis brewing plant. Because the saloonkeepers expressed interest in taking their business outside of Indianapolis to neighboring states, some businessmen saw an opportunity to fill a void and keep the money within the local economy. It was also a way to fight against the English syndicates. Rumors of this new competitive brewery became the talk of the town.

The Home Brewing Company incorporated on June 18, 1891, with the help of ninety local stockholders who invested a total of $200,000 in capital (more than $5 million today). The principal organizer and president was August Hook. Other officers included Andrew Hagen as secretary and treasurer, and later, William P. Jungclaus served as president from 1897 to 1907, while Hook served as vice-president and continued as the company's director of operations. He again became president in 1907 when Jungclaus resigned. Two years later, Hook died suddenly at age sixty of pneumonia on December 10, 1909. His real estate and stock holdings equated to today's equivalent of nearly $2.3 million. Half came from stock in the Home Brewing Company. It was distributed among immediate family members. His son, John Hook, was the founder of the famous Hook's Drugstores.

Active in the community, August Hook belonged to several German organizations including the Indianapolis Liederkranz, a music and singing club created to help preserve German culture and heritage that still operates to this day. He was an immigrant from Viernheim, Germany, and became brewmaster at Lackmann Brewery in Cincinnati, Ohio, before coming to Indianapolis in 1880. He was brewmaster at the Schmidt brewing plant for ten years until he became dissatisfied with the IBC merger.

When a member of the English syndicate learned of the new Home Brewing Company, he immediately started for New York with the remark, "There will be deuce to pay!" They were ready for a fight and sent brewmaster William Gulder from New York to fill the void left by Hook at Schmidt's plant.

The Home Brewing Company laid its cornerstone on September 5, 1891. The new brewery was located at South Cruse and Daly Streets. It

Home Brewing Company. *Indianapolis Public Library.*

was described as a "model of convenience and the arrangements for storing and handling designed to do away with unnecessary labor." At startup, it had thirty-five employees. Its capacity was forty thousand barrels per year—greater than that of Maus's or Lieber's plants and second only to the Schmidt brewery, which had a capacity of sixty thousand, as an article in the paper made sure to mention. It offered a prize of fifty dollars in gold to an artist for the most original and appropriate design of a trademark.

In 1894, the Home Brewing Company announced that it would begin bottling its own brews, which had formerly been bottled by Jacob Bos, who worked in the wholesale wine business and had connections with Hook through the German social clubs. It built a bottling house in proximity to the brewery. An F. Noelxe managed the plant. It had a capacity to bottle twenty barrels daily, delivered for home consumption.

Its brands included Home Brew, Indiana, Pale Select, Stock Ale and Porter. Its popular Columbia brand was touted "queen of table beers." It also brewed Extract of Malt, a medicinal-type beverage. It was advertised as a family blessing and good for children. Pale Select was its top-shelf product, made from German-imported hops and the finest malts. It was only available in bottles.

Under Jungclaus's leadership, the Home Brewing Company expanded a quarter city block and installed an artificial ice machine. In 1904, he made additions to the bottling house, expanding capacity to sixty barrels daily. By the end of his term, the brewery was employing sixty men, producing nearly sixty thousand barrels of beer per year and maintaining twenty-five delivery wagons.

It also sold beer to Jacob Metzger & Company, one of the finest and largest bottling establishments in Indiana. Metzger bottled and sold many well-known brands of both imported and domestic beers. Budweiser, Bass Ale and Guinness Extra Stout were a few examples, as well as ginger ales, blackberry brandies, champagnes and fine wines. The company distributed across Indiana, Ohio, Illinois and Kentucky.

An advertisement for the Home Brewing Company's new Extract of Malt appeared in an 1895 newspaper. It stated that the product is bottled at its bottling department *and* Metzger's bottling plant. This business relationship seemed to be a new development. Also, no other Home Brewing Company advertisements of that kind or quality appeared previously or even subsequently. Interestingly, the ad appeared soon after a falling out between Jacob Metzger and Albert Lieber of the Indianapolis Brewing Company.

Left: Home Brewing Company tray. *The Millers of Greenfield, Indiana.*

Right: Home Brewing Company's Columbia bottle. *The Millers of Greenfield, Indiana.*

Lieber was Metzger's nephew. Metzger had been bottling P. Lieber Brewing Company's beer since 1877. He owned exclusive bottling rights to Lieber's Tafel Beer, which he bottled under the private label "Metzger's Tafel Beer." He also bottled Lieber's Wiener Tafel, Old-Time Ale, Bock and Lager Beer. An 1892 newspaper advertisement proudly stated, "We have, for the last fifteen years, taken rank on all beers in this market. We will continue to hold the same."

However, at some point, Lieber and Metzger had a misunderstanding. Although Lieber insisted on keeping the family matter private, a scandal enflamed gossip among the German circles. An 1895 edition of the *Indianapolis News* indulged one of the stories. Allegedly, a few years prior, Metzger had entertained some British investors visiting Indianapolis and local stockholders in the breweries. During a luncheon, when beer was served, he did not serve an Indianapolis brand, but instead served a St. Louis product. It spiraled into an ongoing feud that culminated in Lieber refusing to sell beer to Metzger. In February the following year, Lieber broke ground on the IBC's new state-of-the-art bottling plant and began bottling its own beer exclusively. He even tried poaching one of Metzger's best employees, offering a higher wage and an enticing incentive. Lieber declined to comment on the story. An 1896 advertisement boasted that Lieber's new bottling plant would increase production from bottling 110 to 140 barrels a day. It also stated that its Tafel Beers not only were sold all over the United States and Canada but also were found on all the Central and South American steamers.

Metzger responded by bottling Lieber's competitor's beer. He made a statement to the *Indianapolis Journal*: "We can only assure our esteemed patrons that we shall now, as ever, provide them with beers equally good, if not better, than those introduced under the well-known brands of 'Metzger's Tafel Beer' and 'Vienna Tafel Beer.'" He later took out another ad citing a steady increase in the demand for the "Original Tafel Beer." He also stated that it was sold by a veteran bottling house and drove the nail in deeper by ending the ad, "We know how to bottle beer."

Metzger threatened to file suit against Lieber for damages. He lost a lot of business, as the IBC products were a major source of revenue. Not to mention he had quite a lot of materials rendered useless. Lucky for him, the Home Brewing Company was open for business.

In 1898, rumors began circulating regarding a purchase offer of the Home Brewing Company. Crawford Fairbanks of the Terre Haute Brewery expressed interest. He seems to have been associated with a Philadelphia syndicate that incorporated in Cincinnati, Ohio. It had $50,000 in capital, with the hopes of controlling the Midwest's beer output. It held options in the Terre Haute Brewing Company and breweries in Lafayette and Fort Wayne. This "malt trust" offered $400,000 for the Home Brewing Company. It was one of eight other breweries. Hagen, the company's secretary and treasurer, asked for more money. The deal fell through the following year when the offer expired. There had been no word from the potential buyers.

Then, in 1901, the HBC made an effort to increase their value and position the brewery for a potential sale. The Home Brewing Company incorporated with the American Brewing Company of Indianapolis. Together, they formed the American Home Brewing Association, with $1 million in stocks. Rumors continued regarding a syndicate purchase and an entirely new Indianapolis brewery. But still, they never found a buyer.

Jacob Metzger & Company (cropped from original image). *Bass Photo Co. Collection, Indiana Historical Society.*

Jacob Metzger bottle, Metzger's Tafel beer glass and Lieber Brewing Company crate, later used by Phoenix Brewing in 1937. *Dave Worthington Collection.*

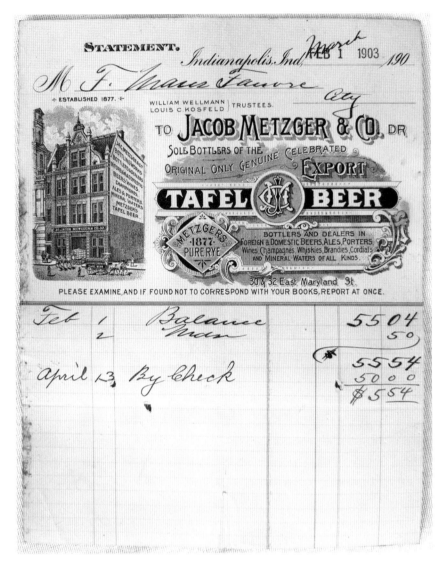

Tafel beer receipt signed by Frank Maus. *The Millers of Greenfield, Indiana.*

Beer profits were not nearly as large as they used to be, pointed out by an anonymous but credible source to the local paper. Congress passed a revenue tax in 1898 to help fund the Spanish-American War. The tax was double for beer at two dollars per barrel, compared to the one-dollar-per-barrel-tax during the Civil War. Organized workers' unions had fought for higher wages in the late nineteenth century, which had also reduced profit margins. By comparison, when the Schmidt, Lieber and Maus breweries were purchased and consolidated for just over $2 million in 1889, their combined annual output was 200,000 barrels of beer. The American Home Brewing Company's combined annual output was only 44,000 barrels, with capital stock of $1 million in 1901.

"Can't you see," concluded the source, "if the Indianapolis Company, with nearly five times the sales, is incorporated for only twice as much as the combined Home and American Companies, it looks as if some mistake has been made?"

The Home Brewing Company had been formed in passionate rebellion against foreign capital. However, perhaps passion and emotion stood in the way of a well-thought-out business decision. According to Albert Lieber, about one year after the HBC began brewing beer, the owners of its capital stock started looking for a way out. They propositioned the English stockholders of the IBC, hoping to get absorbed by the company. However, when the London agents asked for Lieber's referral, he advised against the purchase.

Although the Home Brewing Company couldn't exceed production against its behemoth Indianapolis competitor, these underdog heroes earned their way into the hearts of the community both past and present. In a serendipitous turn of fate, a modern-day craft brewery now occupies the site of the former Home Brewing Company's bottling plant. It is the last standing testament to Indianapolis's pre-Prohibition brewing history. One may visit this local historic treasure at the current Indiana City Brewery located on Shelby Street at the corner of Washington and Southeastern Avenue.

The Godfather of a Brewing Monopoly

"I tell you," whispered the two saloon men at a restaurant, "we've got to do something that will trim Fairbanks and Lieber or we will all be out of business."

"I know it," said the other, "and we have got to get rid of them to save ourselves."

–Indianapolis News, *1907*

The brewing men of the city stood poised—shoulders stiff, fists clenched with adrenaline. Their eyes were intensely focused on the other men across the room who stood equally ready for a fight. It was a standoff at the secret brewers' meeting at the Indianapolis Claypool Hotel during a heated summer in 1907.

Albert Lieber, president of the Indianapolis Brewing Company, raised a chair to strike. Sweat dripped from his forehead onto his perfectly crisp, starched collar. Heat permeated the fine, three-piece woolen suit he'd had tailored at Savile Row during a business trip to London. His vest was tightly buttoned, the last nearly coming undone. His elegantly manicured mustache glistened with perspiration, framing his tightly gripped lips.

"LIAR!" shouted Victor Jose of the Capital City Brewing Company. Albert Lieber lunged toward Jose with his chair raised. Joseph Schaf of the American Brewing Company and others held him back. "Let the coward come," instigated Jose, who then said to Lieber, "You're a liar and a coward or you never would have attempted to play politics with the Council!"

"Shut up," barked Lieber, unyielding.

"I dare you to make me shut up," retorted Jose. Lieber stormed out of the room—furious energy encased in controlled demeanor. He secured his loose button and began plotting his next course of action.

"I will fight this case to the finish," stated Lieber to the local paper. Jose had filed suit against him for slander. Each accused the other of being a liar under the notion that each was trying to ruin the other's reputation. But who was telling the truth?

The trouble between Lieber and Jose started when William A. Heckard, a dentist who had a small stock in the Capital City Brewing Company, demanded to see the list of stockholders, their addresses and number of shares. He insisted on inspecting the books to ascertain the young brewery's financial situation, as was his right as a stockholder. The new company had recently reached its one-year anniversary from the day it incorporated. There had been delays in construction, and allegedly, there was no annual stockholders meeting or election of officers.

Charles Krause, president of Capital City Brewing, refused to show Heckard the books, even though that was against state statute. The problem? He was suspicious of Heckard's relationship with Lieber. His concern was that it may cause some stockholders embarrassment and persecution if the names were made public. Some of Capital City Brewing's stockholders were employees or saloonkeepers who maintained business relationships under the tied-house model with other breweries, including the Indianapolis Brewing Company.

Was a nosey Albert Lieber playing the rules to his advantage? Was he using Heckard as a pawn to gain insider knowledge and control over competition so he could destroy the Capital City Brewery?

Krause stood his ground. Officers of the company were heckled on the streets by constables for not yielding to "Heckard's" demands. The case went to court. Jose testified against Lieber. The judge ruled in Capital City's favor, stating that although the law gave stockholders the right, the circumstances surrounding the case proved in his mind that there was conspiracy against Capital City Brewing. Furthermore, Heckard held the most minimal stock, and the company had even offered to buy him out.

According to a testimony, after the case ruling, Lieber threatened to raise the rent of his saloonkeepers if he found that they had stock in the Capital City Brewing Company. He declared that he would put the brewery out of business. A commenter stated, "We know of no reason by any man wishing to engage in the brewing or any manufacturing business should be compelled to ask permission from Mr. Lieber or anyone else competitively engaged. Mr. Lieber, in this instance, it seems to us, was too greedy. Monopoly is not popular at the present time in Indianapolis or in other cities."

From then on, Jose was adamant that Lieber continued pressing for a way to end Capital City Brewing. In one instance, there was a saloon under indirect control of Lieber, and IBC's beer was sold there exclusively. After Capital tried making a deal with said saloon, suddenly the saloon license was denied by the commissioners due to a "technicality."

One witness claimed that after a man refused to join a plan by Lieber to ruin the brewery, Lieber exclaimed that he would "see the day when he would bend his knee to Albert Lieber."

Capital City refused to cede to Lieber's wishes. The brewery existed as an independent entity, a rebellion against Lieber's monopoly. It seems that he didn't take too kindly to the challenge.

Following the Heckard conspiracy, there was also the matter of Councilman Harry Royse and "the dough." A new ordinance was being considered. It would regulate saloons and give the city council control over granting of licenses. According to rumors, Jose and Royse happened to be riding the same streetcar one day. Jose asked Councilman Royse what he planned to do and why he supported the bill. Royse replied that he was "waiting for the dough." He wanted money to vote against the ordinance. Jose brought this solicitation request before the officers at a brewers' meeting; however, when questioned to the fact, Jose denied any statement to this effect. He never even told anyone about the streetcar conversation. Royse also denied the remark about "the dough."

The case was brought before Fred Eppart, president of the city council. A few days prior, Royse had asked Eppart for a $200 loan for his sick wife.

Albert Lieber. *From Dunn's History of Greater Indianapolis.*

Eppart denied him the loan. He then asked a man by the name of Donovan, and then Donovan solicited the loan from Lieber on Royse's behalf. Lieber said that he thought the situation peculiar. He didn't make the loan because it might cause talk and look bad, especially given the circumstances in the matter of the ordinance. An interesting idea, perhaps?

"I went to Eppart to get even with you," said Lieber to Jose at the Claypool meeting. At least, that was Jose's side of the story. Did Jose and Royse lie to cover up a political misstep? Or was Lieber attempting to spread damaging gossip in an attempt to stay on top?

Albert Lieber enjoyed his status as Indianapolis's brewing royalty. A man of great wealth and influence, he "reveled in his reputation as one of the richest men in the city," as noted in *And So It Goes*. He was well respected among the aristocratic who's who of high society, associating himself with many industrial enterprises and philanthropic endeavors. As a founder of the Commercial Club in 1890, he helped promote a progressive image for the city by advocating for civic improvements and elevating local businessmen to positions of civic and cultural leadership.

An affluent bon vivant, Albert indulged in extravagant luxuries and entertainment and maintained membership in many different social clubs. According to *And So It Goes*, he was the head of a "rich man's club." The initiation rite included blindfolding newcomers and spraying their back sides with beer. Thus, they became official members of the "Wet-Ass" club. One of the members owned the English Hotel and Opera House on Monument Circle. Albert was described as a playboy, and he and his friends would often go there to meet actresses and chorus girls backstage after the show. One source painted Lieber as a narcissistic womanizer who viewed women as merely ornamental.

Lieber had three wives. His first wife, Alice Barus, was an accomplished musician and daughter of a famous choir and symphony conductor. They married in 1887. She died when their three children were very young. Ill-equipped to care for them, Albert rushed into a second marriage with Ora D. Lane, despite warnings from his friends and family. They married in 1900 and divorced in 1912, with Albert alleging cruel and inhumane treatment. Lane was a very attractive, accomplished violinist. Albert's grandson, famed author Kurt Vonnegut Jr., described her as a certified "bat out of hell" who was jealous of Albert's children and abused them. She slept with a loaded pistol under her pillow, claiming that the children were conspiring to harm her. In 1913, he married his third wife, Miss Meda Anne Langtry. She was just slightly older than his firstborn daughter, Edith. They were married until his death.

When Albert's daughter Edith married Kurt Vonnegut Sr., he threw the most spectacular party. According to a biographical sketch, the Vonneguts were considered near the top of the pecking order in the social hierarchy of the community, particularly in the German group. The Liebers and the Vonneguts often rubbed shoulders together as members of Das Deutsche Haus (the current Athenaeum) and vacationed together at their cabins on Lake Maxinkuckee, known as the "Cape Cod of the Midwest."

Albert enjoyed nature and served on the Indianapolis Park Board and the State Department of Conservation. He owned multiple country homes as well as a town house. One included a large country estate in the prestigious Crow's Nest neighborhood just south along Kessler Boulevard. The Vellamada, as he called it, was his four-hundred-acre summer residence overlooking the White River. It included a farm, orchard and hunting grounds.

As much as Albert Lieber was well respected, he was also a ruthless business tycoon, disliked by many. Grandson Kurt Vonnegut Jr. described him as a rascal and emotionally faithless to his children, even going so far as to blame Lieber for his mother's eventual suicide. "I don't think I missed the boat when I failed to write a novel about Albert Lieber," bitterly wrote Vonnegut.

Albert inherited a fortune from his father, Peter, and became even wealthier after the brewery merger. Profit margins were very high for a time. A barrel of beer cost about one dollar to manufacture and sold for about eight. One source claims that he had a cozy relationship with a British representative of the syndicate. They allegedly created special off-the-books accounts for expenditures in order to line their personal pockets, disguising the money as enormous purchases of ice.

According to other sources, Lieber used his money, connections and power to influence politics in his favor. "The public does not know, because the telling of it involves a discussion of subjects not ordinarily thought proper for publication, is that a part of the reward of the brewery man is the right to sell his beer without fear of competition," stated the *Indianapolis News*.

Not only had Lieber gained a monopoly on the state's brewing affairs, but many also felt that he was monopolizing control of public affairs, especially when he formed an alliance with Crawford Fairbanks, who was president of the Terre Haute Brewing Company, and a political ally of Thomas Taggart's. The *Indianapolis News* stated, "The Fairbanks-Lieber policy has been, to be Republican where the Republicans were in power, and Democratic where the Democrats were in power."

Lieber had a reputation to maintain. He was the type of man you didn't want to mess with, especially when it came to his money. He liked being in control and took no qualms reminding those who crossed him just who was in charge. For instance, when the Home Brewing Company, his first competitor, wanted to sell to a syndicate, Lieber, whose opinion was highly valued, refused a good referral. Then there was the Metzger bottling incident, when his uncle served a non-IBC beer to potential investors. Lieber cut business ties and began his own bottling company. He also, allegedly, instigated a warrant against Metzger for acting as an agent for Schlitz without proper license (although he was not technically an agent). Then, two years later, after Jacob Metzger retired, Lieber advocated an ordinance introduced through a councilman who also happened to be an employee of the Indianapolis Brewing Company. The proposed ordinance would have basically singled-out the bottling company and forced them to buy IBC beer from the local beer trust Lieber had established.

There was another case in 1896. An agent for the Cincinnati Brewing Company and vice-president of an ice company wanted to set up shop in Indianapolis. Rumors of a beer war ensued as this new company sold beer to saloonkeepers at $4.50 per barrel. Lieber sold the same for $7.00. He followed the interest closely to make sure that he obtained the required and correct license, although he claimed it didn't make a difference to him. He stated confidently to the paper, "We do not consider the beer he handles as competitive. The beer may be likened to that of Chicago…a city noted for three things; the railroads, the fact the world's fair was held there and for the poor quality of beer manufactured. The Indianapolis Brewing Company does not intend to make this city famous for bad beer. We will continue to manufacture the same quality of beer as in the past and sell it at the same price—$7 a barrel."

One journalist for the newspaper claimed that because the city was indebted to Lieber due to his support in the last campaign, his influence in the city's administration allowed him to sell his beer in "evil resorts." These were disorderly saloons operating without a license.

Lieber donated substantially to the police pension fund. The mayor allowed Lieber, described as the "power behind the administration throne" and the "big boss in local Republican politics," to dictate the makeup of the Board of Public Safety and the police department. He appointed Samuel Gerber as chief detective. Afterward, it was known among saloonkeepers that selling IBC beer ensured a certain type of protection. The police would turn a blind eye. If you didn't, you'd experience their wrath. To make his point, a journalist claiming this story argued that the IBC's sales receipts increased greatly in that first month after the instatement of Gerber as more saloons began selling its beer. As far as saloons operating without a license, IBC would bail them out if they got into any sort of trouble. Sometimes, the bonds remained unpaid.

Just as Lieber started his own bottling company to get back at Metzger, he also had it out for the local distillers and whiskey dealers. He had implemented a working fund on brewers. It was an agreement that all brewers signed (except for Capital City) that acted as a tax to raise money to defeat a high license bill. The distillers refused to contribute money. Lieber punished them by competitively engaging in the wholesale whiskey trade. Regardless, the distillers remained quiet and stayed out of political business. Temperance movements were back on the rise. The whiskey dealers didn't want to further

Men drinking at an Indianapolis tavern, circa 1900. *Indiana Album, the Joan Hostetler Collection.*

arouse public sentiment against the liquor interests. Lieber's connections, political influence, monopoly and share of "evil resorts" contributed in spurring the Indiana temperance movement toward Prohibition.

In 1893, the Anti-Saloon League formed in the neighboring state of Ohio. It had become a national organization by 1895. Following suit, the Indiana branch developed in 1898. The state legislature passed many new, increasingly restrictive prohibition laws in the first decade of the twentieth century. One of those included the 1905 Moore amendment, which strengthened the Nicholson Law of 1895. The Nicholson Law required a two-year waiting period for new licenses. The amendment allowed townships to vote, or remonstrate, against the issuing of licenses, regardless of whether it was a new application or a renewal.

Meanwhile, a few Cincinnati brewery agents came to town. These breweries undercut the Indianapolis breweries by setting up low-cost saloons. Because it seemed that any "Tom, Dick or Harry" could open a saloon, this tended to give rise to some seedy establishments. But it wasn't just the Cincinnati-owned saloons. Some Indianapolis-tied saloons also had reputations for disregarding the rules and contributing to neighborhood riffraff. For a time, Indianapolis had a red-light district.

People began filing general remonstrances to purge their neighborhoods. One disreputable saloon would put an entire district dry. A change was needed. Brewers began feeling a tremendous amount of pressure in an effort to maintain their business. "Unless we organize and elect members of the Legislature who would be friendly to the breweries, the brewery business will be put down and out in Indiana in two years from now," warned Lieber. Jose and other officers of Capital City disagreed—"unless the brewers keep their hands out of politics, they will bring disaster upon themselves."

Lieber organized an Indianapolis Brewers' Exchange during the summer of 1907. It held several meetings to strategize how to save the industry through a Saloon Reformation Agreement. Cutting out objectionable saloons in all parts of the state could solve the problem and gain favor in the eyes of the public, it was thought. At one meeting, Capital City Brewing proposed that they should all agree not to open any more saloons in residential districts. Instead, they would only focus on business districts, figuring it unlikely people would object.

Lieber refused to sign the agreement. Instead, along with Fairbanks, he wanted to section off districts to be controlled by each brewery. If any brewer wanted to open a new saloon in their respective district, they would hold a meeting and it would be approved, or disapproved, through a majority vote.

This was a clever proposal, as the Lieber-Fairbanks alliance held majority vote. Capital City refused to sign that agreement. Then Lieber proposed they all agree to not open anymore saloons at all for the next two years, hoping, perhaps, that temperance movements would calm down by then. This wasn't much of a problem for the established breweries. Was this another scheme to get rid of the newcomer Capital City Brewing? Lieber also later proposed to do away with objectionable saloons. Some believed that it was really a concealed effort to do away with *objectionable competition*.

Lieber stated publicly to the paper that Capital City's proposal was an attempt to "gain the privilege of erecting *so many saloons* in part of the business district and name the boundaries." Capital City felt that the Lieber-Fairbanks proposal was an attempt to limit the capacity for its new business to grow. Lieber denied any sort of split-and-vote proposal against Capital City. He mentioned that Jose came to that meeting with the sole purpose of insulting him and calling him a liar. He then insinuated that Jose fabricated the idea out of paranoia and couldn't understand why Jose believed he was after him.

The saloon reform came to a standstill, as no agreement could be reached. Lieber spun the story to the paper that Capital City was being difficult and was to blame for the lack of progress. All of the other breweries were on board. If Capital had signed it, the reform movement could have started long ago. He made sure to emphasize the fact that he'd been working so hard in favor of temperance, drinking responsibly and in moderation:

> *Beer is absolutely a temperance beverage and statistics prove it so. Brewing is an honorable business. If I didn't think it was I would get out of it at once….The majority of the people are not against alcoholic beverages when they are used temperately* [in moderation], *but they are opposed to them because of the manner in which they are dispensed in many saloons. Knowing this and occupying the position I do in the United States Brewers' Association, I have been identified with the endeavor that has been made among the brewers to conform to the demands of the people. It is for this purpose I have been active in trying to bring about an organization of the brewers that will put the saloons that are objected to on a basis that will meet with the approval of all who are of a practical mind.*

Lieber also tried coercing Capital into contributing money to the brewers' fund to combat the blank remonstrances. He stated that it was their moral obligation to pay into the fund, as all breweries were to profit from it. Jose,

Southside Indianapolis Tavern, circa 1910. *Indiana Album, the Evan Finch Collection.*

still furious about the slander ordeal, refused to pay Lieber. Also, Capital hadn't actually been invited to the meeting where the fund had been discussed, nor had it been invited to join as a member of the exchange. Lieber would not permit it and did not invite Jose to any meetings after the Claypool fight. This didn't sit well with the other breweries in the state, as they "detected a big mouse" in the scheme. Word got out about Lieber's tactics and exclusion of Capital City. Many pulled out, and the Brewers' Exchange fizzled flat, as a commentator stated:

> *When the people learn how Fairbanks and Lieber have been running things they will easily understand why the other brewers are turning from them. Their's is a rule of ruin policy and they make this as effective in politics as in business. If we can break up this influence and eliminate Crawford Fairbanks from the control which, through Tom Taggart, he exercises over the political machine, the brewery business will not be held in the disfavor it now labors under.*

Brewers across the state were beginning to recognize the Lieber-Fairbanks influence over the law and its relation to the rapid advancement of temperance movements in Indiana. They worried that it would mean disaster for the brewing industry, as another commentator noted:

Indiana men with beer, circa 1915. *Indiana Album, the Nancy (Poinsette) DeLullo Collection.*

Among the local breweries, Lieber's influence has long been supreme. But it is believed, now that Jose has broken with him, others will follow and seek to remedy the conditions that have aroused public sentiment against brewery manipulation of public affairs to such a point as to be a real menace to the whole brewery business.

Many citizens sought to purify the legislature by taking down the Fairbanks-Lieber influence. Voting dry meant cutting off their money and, therefore, their power.

That first decade leading to Prohibition was like a pressure cooker for brewers. Blood boiled and tempers rose as their livelihoods came increasingly under threat. Lieber especially had much to lose. He viewed Jose and Capital City Brewing as a pebble in his shoe. Each saw the other as the problem. For a time, the Lieber-Jose drama "threatened to split the brewery business in Indianapolis from here to there."

Eventually, the steam cleared as the two put their differences aside. Jose dropped the charges against Lieber, and all the brewers reached a gentleman's agreement. No brewer was to assist, directly or indirectly, in the erection of any more new saloons for the city of Indianapolis for a period

Albert Lieber's Dark Pretzel Brew. *The Millers of Greenfield, Indiana.*

of two years. They agreed to assist authorities in wiping out saloons of bad character. Thereby, through strict observance of the law, they would gain approval of the citizens. They agreed to not try to step on one another's toes or solicit business away from the other—to cooperate with one another for the greater good of the industry. A white dove of peace had descended on the city's brewers. All was well again, at least for the time being.

THE DARK AGES, 1918-1978

An Irreversible Curse

The American Military Band led a parade of cars the afternoon of April 14, 1905, to the site of a future Capital City Brewery. Two thousand people, officers, directors, stockholders and friends gathered to celebrate the laying of the cornerstone. Charles Krauss, president of the company, gave a happy, welcoming address.

After others presented short speeches, Krauss was presented with a silver trowel to use in setting the stone. Those in attendance created a time capsule with much enthusiasm. They filled a tin box with the daily newspapers of the date and lists of officers and stockholders, as well as a history of the company and other official documents, photographs, a collection of U.S. coins and business cards. Before they sealed the capsule into the cornerstone, Edward Clark, secretary of the Prohibition State Committee, when he thought no one was looking, snuck in this note: "Prohibition will some day close this brewery, and it will be converted into a useful factory, which will be a blessing instead of a curse. And may God hasten the day!" Some brewery men rescued the note from the tin, hoping to reverse the foreshadowing curse, but was it too late? A light began to dim on Indianapolis's golden age of brewing.

Temperance movements were on the rise, gaining in strength and momentum. It was not only a moral issue to prohibitionists but also one of national security, economic necessity, a part of governmental reform and an act of patriotism. The first world war demanded priority over grain for a war-ravaged Europe. People were counting on America to feed them. Many pushed an anti-alcohol agenda under the notion of patriotism. A majority of American brewers were of German descent. Germany became an enemy of the United States, and anti-German sentiments gripped the nation. It didn't look good for German American brewers.

Laws became increasingly restrictive as dry votes swept over Indiana. During the 1908 legislative session, sixty-nine of eighty-two Indiana counties outlawed the sale of alcohol. More than 2,500 saloons closed statewide between 1900 and 1910. As the Anti-Saloon League pushed for nationwide prohibition, Indiana became the twenty-fifth state to enter the movement. The statewide bill took effect on April 2, 1918.

A rainstorm marked the passing of the saloons. The last wet night in Indiana, before the state officially went dry, was unusually quiet. Saloons, hotel bars and private residences across other states who had entered Prohibition threw grand, wild, boozy parties before turning out the lights. Spirits in Indiana, however, seemed dampened due to the rain and the war.

Nationwide Prohibition officially took effect on January 17, 1920. Those who supported the new legislation had high hopes for the social, moral and economic fabric of society. However, enforcing the amendment proved difficult. Some argue that the implementation of the "Noble Experiment" resulted in even more disastrous consequences. Underground crime increased as an unregulated industry set the stage for lucrative business opportunities. The court system overflowed with Prohibition violators. Many states lost major sources of revenue from excise taxes on liquor sales. "At the national level, Prohibition cost the federal government a total of $11 billion in lost tax revenue, while costing over $300 million to enforce," according to Lerner's article "Prohibition" on PBS. The rise in predicted alternative industries and economic benefits did not come to pass. Thousands lost their jobs, including those in related trades like barrel-makers, truckers and restaurant staff.

Alcohol consumption also skyrocketed. Consumers found ways to satisfy their boozy desires. Many breweries began making malt extract products with clever "warning labels" that people used to illegally brew beer at home. Some bootleggers inadvertently created poisonous libations that sometimes proved fatal. The quality of alcohol on the black market declined. An average of one thousand American fatalities occurred each year from the effects of drinking tainted liquor. For the Indianapolis breweries that clung to manufacturing alternative products, it was just a matter of time.

Putting Indiana in the country's "dry" column. Indiana, 1917. *Library of Congress.*

"We Want Beer." Soldiers return from World War I, 1919, Indiana. *Indiana Red Cross and the IUPUI University Library Digital Collections.*

Capital City Brewing struggled even before Prohibition. Some sources claim that it was mismanaged. Industry changes had caused profit margins to drop. There was also more competition, and the marketplace was oversaturated with saloons, some of which bolstered temperance laws due to their objectionable character. Starting a new brewing venture in an anti-saloon climate leading up to Prohibition probably wasn't the best move.

In 1913, it was revealed that Capital City had not been paying dividends, and the company reorganized with new officers. The following year, a stockholder sued the brewery, claiming that the company was loaning money to illegal saloons, wasting resources, infringing on other breweries' trademarks, deceiving stockholders and paying out dividends on borrowed money. The suit was filed on behalf of the stockholder by Victor Jose Jr., son of the former manager and secretary of Capital City Brewing, who left during the reorganization to manage the Schlitz Brewing Company branch in Indianapolis.

In 1915, a receiver of Capital City Brewing disposed of the brewery to an attorney representing anonymous buyers. The plant was appraised at $140,000 and sold at a high bid of $135,700. The once confident start-up company never reached its seventy-five-thousand-barrel annual capacity. It was assumed that the general creditors would probably not realize anything on their claim.

The next day's paper unveiled that a new brewing company had purchased the Capital City property: Citizen's Brewing Incorporated, with former officer Charles Krauss named as president. It made Peerless Citizen's beer. During Prohibition, it converted to cold storage and curing meat for export. The building also served as a branch of the Polk Sanitary Milk Company used for cold storage and creamery purposes. The old brewing equipment was packed up and shipped to Japan.

The American Brewing Company saw the writing on the wall. Joseph Schaf sold an option on the brewery in 1911 to John J. Giesen, former brewmaster and vice-president of Capital City Brewing. It appears that Giesen sold his stock and got out of the company after Capital City's stock value suddenly jumped several points in January that year. There had been rumors of merging with the Home Brewing Company that created heavy

Citizens Brewing beer tray. *The Millers of Greenfield, Indiana.*

demand for the stock. Giesen partnered with a few local hotel men. They incorporated with $200,000 in capital stock as the John J. Giesen Brewing Company and worked a deal to purchase the American Brewing Company's plant for $375,000. Schaf made plans to retire. However, the deal fell through, and Giesen was not expected to live as the result of a troublesome affair with near fatal results.

Giesen found himself in financial ruin. His mistress, Miss Jennie Barlow, expressed desire to leave the city and discontinue their years-long illicit relationship. One night, an intoxicated Giesen went to Barlow's apartment at 228 West Michigan Street. Angry words spiraled into a heated lovers' quarrel. Giesen allegedly drank poison, shot his mistress and then shot himself in a suicide attempt. Both ended up unconscious and in the hospital with severe bullet wounds. Barlow suffered a bullet through her back and into her left lung. Giesen bore scratches on his face along with two bullet wounds to his chest just below the heart. Although he denied it, according to a statement by the hospital, his tongue appeared burnt from drinking mercury bichloride. It's possible that he mistook the poison for whiskey, as the two bottles looked similar and were positioned next to the other at the mistress's home.

Barlow claimed that Giesen had attacked her. When she broke away and turned for the door, he shot her and then turned the gun on himself. He insisted that she shot first with the revolver he had given her as a gift some time ago and then shot herself. The hospital told Giesen that he was unlikely to survive, to which he replied, "I'm too tough to die." Both lingered between life and death but survived. Barlow was charged with assault and battery, Giesen with assault and battery with intent to kill.

The American Brewing Company filed articles of dissolution in February 1918, just before statewide prohibition took effect. It removed the machinery. The building remained idle until a transportation company purchased it as a terminal for freight truck deliveries. Joseph Schaf later leased the building to a supply firm at $794,000 for a ninety-nine-year term.

A tax assessment in 1919 showed that the Home Brewing Company's valuation dropped from $37,000 to $4,000 from the year prior. It fought against the new "dry law" along with others, who argued the Beebe case from 1855. Preventing it from doing business was against its constitutional rights, contended the HBC. It asked for a temporary injunction to prevent the prohibition enforcement, asserting that it had invested $600,000 into the company and that the charter it held with the state to do business was a valid contract. Enacting the law would impair the obligation of the contract. Its attempts returned unsuccessful. Even though the new legislation tied its hands and pushed it toward insolvency, the court ordered the Home Brewing Company to continue paying on a five-year saloon lease. The Superior Court ruling was that all brewing companies were bound by leases of real estate made before the enforcement of the prohibition law.

The Home Brewing Company crawled along making "near beer," which was common for many breweries during Prohibition. This beer was permissible by law, as it contained less than 0.5 percent alcohol. The Home Brewing Company's "homo" beer, as it called it, was as close to the genuine, old style of beer as possible. The best substitute during the "Bone Dry" period, it claimed. However, in 1918, Indiana limited the manufacture of near beer to 1.5 million barrels per year. The order was designed to conserve coal during the war. This allotment between the state's thirty breweries represented about 50 percent of their normal output.

The Home Brewing Company tried making do with a small soda manufacturing plant. It also continued producing its Extract of Malt but faced legal trouble. Someone filed a petition against it, claiming that the malt and hop compound was used by individuals to make beer at home. Although the Home Brewing Company won the case, as the product was within the provisions of the law, it couldn't sustain the business.

The Home Brewing Company closed its doors by 1920. The main plant later accommodated the Indianapolis Power and Light Company radio station and was also used by the Motor Transit Management Company to operate the Greyhound and Pickwick bus lines. The building was remodeled for storage and manufacturing purposes in 1928. It has since been demolished. The remaining bottling plant became home to the Majestic Tire and Rubber Company. For a time, the government used the remainder of the building to store automobiles. It was later leased to several different concerns.

One by one, what remained of the brewing industry in Indianapolis began to crumble—bottles of beer confiscated by police, buildings abandoned, equipment liquidated, brewery fixtures at saloons gutted and thousands of jobs lost. The last man standing was Albert Lieber.

Leading up to Prohibition, the Indianapolis Brewing Company remained relatively strong. In 1914, it had 500 employees, 210 head of horses and 9 automobiles and produced an average of 30 million bottles of beer per year. Lieber had always been a man who supported temperance,

Lieber's Gold Medal Cereal Beverage. Indianapolis Brewing Company, Prohibition era. *The Millers of Greenfield, Indiana.*

or drinking responsibly and in moderation. Even before Prohibition, the Indianapolis Brewing Company made temperance products called Tonica and Ozotonic. Tonica was available in light or amber. These were low-alcoholic malt beverages often marketed as medicinal products. You could even give them to your baby, it was claimed. A 1918 newspaper advertisement boasted, "To Indianapolis must again go the credit for leading the country…no city in America has been working so long, so intelligently and so effectively on a pure cereal beverage.…Tonica is America's Ideal Beverage."

During Prohibition, the Indianapolis Brewing Company chugged along, making its Tonica and Gold Medal Cereal Beverages. It also made carbonated beverages, malt syrup, soft drink syrups and various sodas like Cher-ay, Lime Cola and Ginger Ale. Lieber's Root Beer was available on draft at soft drink parlors or in bottles.

But the business struggled, a shell of its former glory. By 1919, the brewery was employing just fifteen persons. One of the three plants was in use, while the others remained idle. Lieber slowly began closing and consolidating properties. The idle buildings were sold for storage or for industrial use. An ice company took over one of the branches. He closed a portion of the Schmidt plant in 1918. The remaining space manufactured soda until 1920, when production was abandoned completely and soda production was transferred to the Lieber branch. IBC limped along with one remaining plant.

The Vonnegut Hardware Company later used the abandoned Schmidt complex as a warehouse. In 1926, Josiah K. Lilly purchased the once-famous Schmidt's Square to use as space for his grandfather's pharmaceutical firm, Eli Lilly and Company, as noted in the *Indianapolis News*: "The deal marks the passing into history of an old landmark of the activities of a former day…It is said to be worthless for any use." The brewery, touted in its glory days as the best in the West, was razed and turned to dust.

Albert Lieber, once relentless in his business pursuits, had retired by 1931. He was around the age of seventy and spent his remaining years in travel. Illness struck him the year Prohibition was repealed. He passed away the following year in September 1934. The fires under the brew kettles were reduced to smoldering embers. It would be many decades until Indianapolis would experience a great brewing revival with the coming of the American craft beer revolution.

Out with the Old, In with a Scandal

The smell of cracked grain permeated the frozen air. One by one, the brew kettles fired back up. Hot liquor raced through the old pipes, spilling gleefully into the mash tubs. Brewers poured over pages filled with retired recipes.

Repeal came with the Twenty-First Amendment, fully ratified on December 5, 1933. The brewing industry forever changed. Many breweries didn't survive Prohibition. Then there was economic collapse and the Second World War. Larger breweries eventually swallowed up the smaller operations. Following World War II came a new, modern era of explosive economic growth and innovation in the United States. The past was left behind. All eyes were on a bright, new future as Big Beer superseded the brewing industry.

Many factors played a role in the development of large-scale commercial brewing in a postwar booming economy. Mass production technology improved and allowed for greater output. There was growth in transportation, roadways and trucking. Distribution became easier

Indianapolis Brewing Company workers packaging Gold Medal October Ale, circa 1930s–1940s. *Indiana Historical Society, P0569.*

and more widespread. The 1950s saw an increase in media technology. Television and radio became readily available to the masses. This meant more marketing opportunities. Because media outlets were typically limited to three channels, there was less competition for consumer attention and more focused messaging. Advertising was a cutthroat business. The beer industry saw a shift, with more focus and effort on marketing and less on quality of products. Make it, sell it, ship it—tied up with a nice little ribbon. Large-scale commercial brewing thrived in a consumer/packaged goods model. Gone were the days of traditional, old-world brewing.

Before the official repeal of Prohibition, brewers old and new geared up brewing equipment, ready to brew in anticipation of a new era. In Indianapolis, several companies attempted to revive the Indianapolis Brewing Company, or at least pay homage to the bygone brewing giant.

Leo C. McNamara, son of a former employee at the old Maus plant, was now president of the newly formed Indiana Breweries Inc. George J. Steinmetz was vice-president. They had purchased the plant in 1922 and patiently waited ten years until they were finally able to begin

Opposite, top: Indianapolis Brewing Company chemist working. Gold Medal beer sits on table, circa 1930s–1940s. *Indiana Historical Society, P0569.*

Opposite, bottom: Indianapolis Brewing Company kegs. *Indiana Historical Society, P0569.*

Above: Mausner Lager wagon, circa 1930s. *Bass Photo Co. Collection, Indiana Historical* Society.

manufacturing. They cleaned the cobwebs and fired up the brew kettles at the old Maus brewery. Since making alcohol was still technically illegal, they brewed liquid malt until they received an amended permit that allowed them to turn it into beer.

Their first product was a new beer called Mausner, a tribute lager brewed "like the old days" by none other than brewmaster John Giesen (formerly associated with the Indianapolis Brewing Company, then the Capital City Brewery; then he tried to start his own brewing company and then drank poison, got shot, tried to kill his mistress and nearly died—he really *was* tough!). He had also formed the Giesen Products Company in 1926 during Prohibition. His company bottled carbonated beverages and manufactured soft drinks at the Lieber plant of the Indianapolis Brewing Company. This man just wouldn't quit.

Giesen's Mausner was the first locally produced beer to go on the Indianapolis market since Prohibition and was featured as the exclusive beer of the state fair. Indiana Breweries Inc. also made several other brands of beer, including the first seasonal bock beer since Prohibition and a pilsner called Indiana Club. The pilsner was brewed using the world's finest Saaz hops from Czechoslovakia. Another notable brand was Cream Velvet, a beer the Terre Haute Brewing Company took issue with because it felt the trademark name infringed on its Champagne Velvet brand.

Indiana Breweries Inc. later reincorporated as the Indianapolis Brewing Company Inc., with William E. Clauer as the new president. The Indianapolis Brewing Company was back! (Sort of.) In 1936, it spent $125,000 to increase output and ranked among the four leading breweries of the state.

The International Brewing Company incorporated in the summer of 1933. A fire thwarted its efforts to renovate the old IBC's Lieber plant. Flames swept through the building, causing considerable damage. It also had trouble obtaining a brewing permit, as there were only a certain number allowed in the state.

A few months later, it merged with another brewing effort, the General Brewing Corporation. Together they formed the Gold Medal Brewing Company and were able to obtain the twenty-second and last available brewery permit in the state. Notable officers included Frank W. Hoch as president and Anton Kainz as vice-president. Hoch's family, according to the newspaper announcement, was the first to introduce bottled beer in America and was well connected to the brewing industry many years prior to Prohibition. Kainz was a native of Munich, Germany. A job at the Fortune Brothers Brewing Company of Chicago brought him to the States. At the time, he was considered an authority on both domestic and foreign brews. The new Gold Medal Brewing Company hired the former chief engineer and brewmaster of the old Indianapolis Brewing Company, Louis C. Reifeis.

The following year, they continued the remodel of the Lieber plant and installed large orders of brand-new, state-of-the-art equipment. A year later, the Gold Medal Brewing Company went bankrupt, and the company disappeared. In 1938, plans were underway to convert the Lieber plant into an industrial complex called the Madison Avenue Industrial Center.

In 1933, a Midwest Brewing Company took over Citizen's Brewing (formerly the old Capital City Brewery). That same year, a man from Indy's famous brewing family entered the picture. Colonel Richard Lieber was Peter Lieber's nephew and cousin of Albert Lieber.

Richard Lieber at Turkey Run State Park. *Indiana State Library.*

Like Albert, Richard Lieber was a very prominent and influential man with interests in civic affairs. He was listed in the *Who's Who of America* and is most noted as the "Father of the Indiana State Parks System" through his work in conservation of natural resources. He advocated the creation of state parks and succeeded in buying land for Turkey Run and McCormick's Creek largely from private donations. His method for building parks became a model for the rest of the United States. "Indiana's State Park system is regarded as the best in the country," stated a 1944 edition of the *Indianapolis News*, "and its excellence is attributed largely to [Richard Lieber's] pioneer work."

In 1933, a new Democratic governor discontinued the Conservation Commission. A frustrated Richard Lieber resigned as the director of Indiana's Department of Conservation, a position he had held since 1919. He turned his attention, instead, to brewing. Richard bought into the Midwest Brewing Company, renaming it the Richard Lieber Brewing Corporation and later, in 1934, the Lieber Brewing Corporation. His philosophy was quality over quantity, as he told the *Indianapolis Star*: "Having devoted my entire time for fourteen years to a type of public service which I hope has beneficially influenced the mode of living of many citizens in the state of Indiana. I feel that by accepting the position of president and manager of this new enterprise, I may continue to be of service to the public."

Also, like Albert, Richard Lieber was a man who supported temperance: "The beverage industry has a function of its own to perform and must participate in all educational movements which will bring about a sane, temperate and proper use of beverages with alcoholic content. The beer industry is particularly interested because beer is a food product, beneficial to mankind when properly used."

Although Richard Lieber didn't have direct experience in the manufacturing of beer, he did own a bottling company. Established in 1896 and bankrolled by his cousin Albert Lieber, the Richard Lieber & Company bottled various beverages like wine, cordials, whiskey, sodas and mineral and medicinal waters. The company also worked to supply Indianapolis with pure and sterilized water. It was located on the corner of New York and Agnes Streets—the same location as Maus's brewery. Frank Maus had helped found the American Brewing Company in 1897 and turned more of his attention to this endeavor. It's likely that Albert Lieber made room for his cousin's company at the Maus plant.

Richard Lieber's new brewing company reconditioned the old Capital City Brewery, once his cousin's sworn enemy, into a modern and efficient manufacturing facility. It was soon recognized as one of the most up-to-date in the nation.

Fred E. Hoermann was the head brewmaster and superintendent. His father was a renowned brewmaster from Bavaria, where Hoermann learned the trade as a young boy. He also studied at the Royal Brewers and Agricultural Academy in Weihenstephan and the University of Munich, majoring in chemical engineering and fermentation. After graduating, he became assistant brewer at various breweries in Bavaria, Switzerland and France. When he came to America, he served as an instructor at a brewers' school in New York. Later, he became brewmaster at the Gambrinus Brewery in Columbus, Ohio, and other breweries throughout the states. When the United States adopted the Eighteenth Amendment, Hoermann took his profession to Mexico and Canada before returning and taking the position at Richard Lieber's brewery. All the other men connected with the brewery were old-time brewery employees long active in the industry before Prohibition.

After Albert Lieber passed away in 1934, Richard Lieber's brewery began brewing Lieber Lager in honor of the Lieber family heritage. It debuted on April 25, 1935, with outpouring support from the community and local businesses.

Demand for Lieber Lager grew steadily and substantially. In 1935, the brewery began an expansion project to double production capabilities with plans to distribute beyond Indianapolis. Local architectural firm Vonnegut, Bohn & Mueller designed the new structure. Most of what remained of the old building was in poor condition, save three walls. It demolished the rest.

As much as Richard Lieber's brewery tried to bring hope and prosperity to Indianapolis, the United States was still recovering from the Great Depression, and the threat of World War II loomed in the distant future. The reemerging beer industry struggled.

Colonel Lieber returned to his work in conservation. From 1939 to 1944, he

Advertisement for Lieber Lager, circa 1930s. *The Millers of Greenfield, Indiana.*

served as chairman of the board of the National Conference on State Parks. He also worked as an advisor for the National Park Service for many years.

Richard Lieber's brewery fell into receivership and was sold to the recently organized Phoenix Brewing Corporation in 1937. Officers included former officers of the Lieber Brewing Corporation. Theirs were the only bid, and they planned to recommence brewing the first day of January the following year. Appointed to the general manager position was John L. Reuss. He was the grandson of the founder of Fort Wayne's Centlivre Brewing Company, where he acted as secretary, advertising manager and director.

The company soon reincorporated as Ajax Brewing. It hired a well-known brewmaster by the name of Jacob Guehring, who began brewing on January 3, 1938. Beer would be available by April after ninety days of aging. Guehring had more than forty years' experience. He began brewing at age fourteen in Chicago with his father. He later studied in Munich, Germany, and brewed at various breweries across the United States. As Reuss declared in an announcement:

> *The management considers itself quite fortunate in having been able to secure a man of such capabilities as Mr. Guehring. I have received numerous and hearty congratulatory expressions on his ability from individuals and companies long identified with the industry….It is the aim and intent of the Ajax Brewing Corporation to produce a product of which Indianapolis may be proud.*

Ajax Brewing took great pride in manufacturing affordable, consistent, high-quality, all-grain beer with choice hops from Oregon and the finest imported from Bohemia. An "Ajax Quality Seal of Approval" went on every bottle. It brewed Ajax Beer, marketing it cleverly with "'X' Marks the Spot." In addition, it brewed a beer with a name slightly familiar to the old Indianapolis Brewing Company: Düselager, "the best beer brewed in the middle west with real, old-fashioned flavor." Ajax became most noted for its Imperial Select Pale Ale. This was its premium, luxury product brewed for winter consumption. However, it advertised that it could be enjoyed all year round. It was heavy in body with a pale, dry flavor. Customers agreed that it was one of the best domestic beers and compared favorably with some imports. A company official noted, "There are good reasons for this. Imperial is a 'pet' product of a brewmaster of the old school, with experience here and abroad, a man whose forefathers have been brewmasters for generations. The secrets of the trade have been handed down father to son."

Even Imperial's bottle and label design received accolades from several industrial artists, and so the company entered the bottle into the American Packaging Exposition in New York.

Sales grew, and Indianapolis welcomed the new industry as much needed, bringing more jobs and opportunity to the city. The brewery anticipated an increase in sales for 1939 to result in a 40 percent growth in staffing. Later that year, Reuss resigned and returned to Centlivre Brewing. E. Arthur Ball of Ball Brothers Company in Muncie took his place. Then, in 1940, the short-lived Ajax Brewery went up for sale. That left one Indianapolis brewery remaining: the Indianapolis Brewing Company.

In 1945, the Bardin brothers, of Milwaukee breweries, purchased the Indianapolis Brewing Company from William Clauer. Alvin Bardin was president and his brother, Archie Bardin, vice-president. They purchased the old Maus plant for $500,000 and planned a $200,000 expansion, anticipating a market increase due to the lifting of wartime restrictions.

The former owner had been brewing Gold Medal Beer, a line that included a lager, a bock and an October ale. Although these were popular among Indiana locals, the new ownership at first planned to substitute its own brands but later realized the error, stating, "They are a part of Indianapolis and are here to stay." The third brother, Lawrence Bardin, moved to Indianapolis to oversee the new operation as general manager. He reassured IBC fans that he would continue satisfying demand with these products.

Then, in 1946, just after the war, President Truman announced a plan encouraging restrictions on wheat for brewing and distilling as part of his bread-for-Europe program. He also limited the amount of other grains for said purposes. Bardin responded, "The order banning the use of wheat will have no effect here, as this company uses no wheat in making its Gold Medal Beer, which is made of corn, barley, malt and hops. However, the limiting of other grains to 1940 levels…as well as an expected cut in the use of malt, will curtail beer production by 20 percent from the annual output of 125,000 barrels."

Over the course of the next several months, the Indianapolis Brewing Company came unraveled, revealing a scandal. Two separate companies sued the IBC for failure to deliver on contracts that year. One claimed $20,000 in damages over an unfulfilled order. The company sent empty bottles to be filled by the IBC, and the brewery owed it 14,977 cases of beer. The other claimed $113,200 in a similar suit. IBC's secretary and treasurer blamed the grain and subsequent beer shortage but refused to return the bottles or issue a refund.

A few months later, Centlivre Brewing in Fort Wayne issued the IBC an order to cease and desist. It filed a claim of $50,000 in damages for a trademark infringement over its "Old Crown" beer after IBC filed a trademark for "Crown Select." It was a huge blow to IBC. Although it struggled financially, to the public, it appeared that the brothers were extremely successful. In addition to it being the fourth-largest brewery in Indiana, their personal assets included three private airplanes, thirteen automobiles and four trucks.

A truer picture caught up with Lawrence the following year when the government claimed $483,096.33 against him in unpaid federal income tax for 1946. That would be equal to nearly $7 million today. Lawrence's brother, Archie, reported $250,000 in large bills stolen from his Los Angeles home earlier that May. The robbery occurred the same day Lawrence filed his income tax return in Indianapolis. The money had been taken there by Lawrence in his personal airplane and kept in a private safe. He claimed that he was saving it for his income tax payments.

A federal court ordered a seizure of the brewery as well as the brothers' Marion County properties, but the IBC was able to avert the seizure with negotiations. They were, however, ordered a restraint, limiting them to "normal business" transactions. While the IRS computed tax claims, Lawrence was removing his properties out of the state. He also closed a stock account, converted it to cash and removed the money to places unknown.

In addition to the federal tax lien against Bardin, there was also a federal tax lien against the Indianapolis Brewing Company for $612,086.99 for fraudulent intent to cheat the government out of its claim. The lien cited alleged unpaid corporate income and/or excess profits taxes for 1945 and 1946. This boosted federal claims against the company to more than $1 million.

As well as tax evasion claims, there was also a civil suit claiming $556,607 for over-the-ceiling beer price violations and a criminal count for short-filling bottled beer. Bardin was selling bottled beer one ounce below the amount of the twelve-ounce label. The company collected $177,689 in overcharges.

In total, the IBC bore claims in excess of the brewery's worth. A judge deemed the heavily indebted brewery insolvent because of overdrafts on bank accounts and its inability to obtain loans. During an IBC receivership hearing, the company was charged with violating its federal restraining order. It had purchased a brand-new Cadillac for one of its officers. The brewery owned four Cadillacs. One of the luxury automobiles was driven by Lawrence, who was no longer employed by the brewery.

The Indianapolis Brewing Company entered into a receivership and, in November 1947, was ordered to stop brewing. A witness testified that the brewery had a backlog of 5,800 barrels of beer on hand but slow sales. It also stated that the company's sales decreased with loss of the U.S. Navy business and loss of a local market for its product Crown Select. Brewing was halted indefinitely.

Lawrence Bardin was arrested in 1948 for short-filling bottles. He was to serve a six-month sentence. He wanted to go in style. As an aviation enthusiast, he asked to be flown to prison in a private airplane and even offered to pay all the expenses. He still owed the lien on his 1946 federal income taxes. Lawrence went to jail by car, same as the other criminals.

Later, in 1953, Lawrence was sentenced to a four-year term for tax evasion. During the trial, witnesses testified claiming deals made under the table. Some said that they were required to buy stock in the company in order to make purchases and then Bardin would buy the stock back at a lower price. Bardin's defense was that he was an employee of the brewery and not personally responsible for the profits.

Soon, Bardin was out on bond. However, two weeks later, he was back in jail after an irate bondsman discovered that he had been furnished a bad check forged by Bardin under his brother Alvin's name. The bounced check led to Bardin, who was found living in a swanky Chicago hotel.

The Indianapolis Brewing Company scandal was a national news sensation and received much criticism for its connections in politics after it settled an $812,000 tax bill for $4,500 in cash. It settled the $556,607 civil suit for $50,000. Some criticized the fact that Frank McKinney, chairman of the Democratic National Committee, helped finance the brewery purchase in 1945. The IBC also received a $35,000 refund with help from its attorney, Joseph D. Nunan Jr. He served as commissioner of internal revenue from 1944 to 1947 and also later went to prison himself for tax evasion. Lawrence Bardin's defense for his personal tax case, he believed, was that the settlement with the IBC relieved him of any personal obligation. He contended that the government was trying to collect twice because it was forced to make a bad settlement.

An attorney and investor purchased the Indianapolis Brewing Company in 1948 at a $105,000 bid with plans to lease the building. He outbid Alvin Bardin. It would be forty years before the city saw another brewery. The lit match that guided Indy into a golden age of brewing reached the end of its trail. With one last flicker, it choked out, leaving behind a void of ash, smoke and black.

• Part II •

Modern Craft Beer in Indianapolis, 1978–2022

DAWN OF HOMEBREWING, BREWPUBS AND EVANGELICALS, 1978-2008

OUT OF THE ASH

The unmistakable crack of a beer cap releasing a bottle's pent-up carbonation broke the silent darkness in 1989. Main Street Lager was the first beer brewed in Indianapolis in more than forty years. Like a phoenix rising from the ashes, the Indianapolis Brewing Company reemerged into a modern era.

It was the beginning of a renaissance, an era marked by small-scale production breweries and the rise of hand-crafted, artisanal ales—a movement known as the American craft beer revolution. Craft beer was just beginning to emerge in the Midwest, and the reinvented Indianapolis Brewing Company joined the microbrew craze. The East and West Coasts already enjoyed a sprinkling of established brewpubs and microbreweries. In 1983, there were between ten and fifteen microbreweries in the United States. By the time the Indianapolis Brewing Company opened, that number had grown to more than two hundred.

Big Beer reigned during most of the mid-twentieth century. That "yellow fizzy stuff" produced for the masses at macrobreweries dominated liquor store shelves and draft lines, along with a growing trend toward imports. Then Jack McAuliffe founded New Albion Brewing in Sonoma County, California, in 1976. It's credited as the first U.S. microbrewery of the modern era—a blueprint paving the way for small-scale production breweries.

Throughout most of the 1980s and early '90s, craft beer represented less than 1 percent of the beer market share with a slow, steady increase. Then, in 1995, that number jumped to 2 percent. By 2005, craft beer represented more than 3 percent and was growing. By 2019, according to the Brewer's Association, there were 8,391 craft breweries, which included 1,821 microbreweries, 3,171 brewpubs, 3,159 taprooms and 240 regional craft breweries. Retail dollar value was estimated at $29.3 billion, representing 25.2 percent market share.

In 1987, Thomas Peters and Richard Harris, Indianapolis restaurant professionals and beer aficionados, decided to try and capitalize on the industry trend. Through a combination of borrowed funds, secondhand equipment and capital stock sold mostly to friends and family, the pair launched Nap Town Brewing in February 1989, pioneering a new frontier in Indiana. As Peters stated in the *Tipton County Tribune*, "We're the only microbrewery in the state and a lot is brand new. We don't know what to expect."

Inspired by California brewpubs and after researching their idea in Boston, they set up shop at an Eastside industrial park located at 3250 North Post Road. Harris recalled to a local paper, "I thought if restaurants can brew their own beer and sell it, I figured we can brew our own beer for the restaurants and sell it to them."

Neither had experience in brewing. They read books, homebrewed and gathered advice from experienced brewers. Part of their quest included time spent volunteering and learning to brew with Indianapolis native Jamie Emerson at his Hood River brewery in Oregon.

The rookie brewers began brewing their first batch of Main Street Lager on January 20, 1989. It was an amber-colored, Munich-style lager with a richer flavor and fuller body than most domestics. They brewed on a twenty-barrel system with forty-barrel fermenters to produce two thousand to three thousand barrels per year. By mid-March, Main Street Lager was heading for distribution to eighteen Indianapolis restaurants. These included St. Elmo's, Ale Emporium, Pawn Shop, Union Jacks Pub in Broad Ripple, the Elbow Room and Rick's Café.

Beaming with hope and anticipation for a bright future, the duo shared their passion by giving brewery tours two Saturdays a month. Visitors learned about the brewing process and sampled beer at different stages. The brewery did not have a taproom. It was strictly a production facility for distribution only, a place of industry, open Monday through Friday from seven o'clock in the morning until five in the evening.

About a year later, after much foam and sparkling enthusiasm, sales fizzled flat. It was back to the drawing board. Peters and Harris acquired rights to the old Indianapolis Brewing Company, donated by a retired president of the Pepsi-Cola Bottling Company who dropped his plans to open a brewpub. Intent on reviving a piece of history, Nap Town Brewing rebranded in 1990 to keep the tradition alive. The Indianapolis Brewing Company experienced a rebirth, one hundred years after its inception.

They hired Kim Renfro as general manager, consulted a brewmaster from Molson Beer and hired brewmaster John Battles. They redesigned labels, tweaked the old Main Street Lager recipe and increased marketing efforts. They emulated pre-Prohibition lagers and added more variety to their offerings. These included a pilsner, a pale ale, an Oktoberfest, a barrel-aged stout, a winter bock and other seasonal brews. They brought back a version of the famous Duesseldorfer in pale, amber and dark. Duesseldorfer Draft Ale became their specialty, and Brick Yard Bock had staying power. On October 18, 1994, they released a special Duesseldorfer Amber Ale. It was only available locally in twenty-two-ounce bottles—a tribute to an Indianapolis Brewing Company original.

The new recipes gained in popularity. The company expanded and distributed to more than two hundred Indianapolis bars and restaurants and to retail outlets like Kahn's Fine Wines and Spirits. It sold beer at the RCA Dome and distributed to fourteen states, as well as Japan and England. It also contract-brewed for the Kentucky Brewing Company of Lexington; the Fort Wayne Brewing Company; Pike Place in Seattle, Washington; San Juan of Telluride, Colorado; Pacific Hop Exchange in California; and Beer Across America, a beer-of-the-month club.

Then, in 1997, the company dissolved. As Peters explained in Douglas A. Wissing's book *One Pint at a Time*, "It was a struggle in the middle of light-beer country. We were stuck in no-man's land—too big to be low-cost and too small for economies of scale."

"It opened some eyes," continued Peters, "made people more adventuresome. It was a fun way to make a living for a while."

The modern-day Indianapolis Brewing Company was the first microbrewery in Indiana. Although it pioneered a new frontier during the craft beer movement, it was not the first to bring craft beer to the state. The Broad Ripple Brewpub was the first brewpub and craft brewery, followed by Sun King as the first production craft brewery.

Microbreweries led the forefront of craft brewing, while "craft brewery" is a relatively recent concept. The former relates more to size, while the latter relates more to brewing technique. A microbrewery is defined as producing fewer than fifteen thousand barrels of beer per year and sells 75 percent or more of its beer off-site. A craft brewery is small and independently owned, typically producing less than larger breweries. It takes an artisanal approach, with a hallmark for innovation. A craft brewery doesn't necessarily indicate a microbrewery, and microbreweries may or may not brew craft beer. Considered an art by brewmasters, some may argue that more heart and soul goes into making a craft beverage.

"Microbrewery" and "craft brewery" typically fall under the umbrella of being production breweries—meaning that they mainly brew beer to distribute off-premises. (However, not all craft breweries are production breweries.) In addition, these may also offer connected tasting rooms or taprooms for visitors. Rarely is there food service, although some maintain outside food vendors like food trucks, casual food stalls within the tasting room or other food service contracted with separate companies.

Brewpubs, on the other hand, are restaurants that brew their own beer for serving primarily on-premises. Although they may sell beer to go and/or in some cases distribute to off-site accounts, generally they do not bottle or distribute. One usually must visit the brewpub in order to drink its beer. By nature, brewpubs include a craft brewery.

Brewpubs were on the rise in Indianapolis during the 1990s. This was also a time when a dilapidated downtown Indianapolis began to experience a resurgence. Revitalization projects like the addition of sports venues, the Circle Center Mall, the White River State Park and other cultural developments, as well as brewpubs, made downtown Indy a destination for food, shopping and entertainment. It was no longer a place where the sidewalks rolled up at 5:00 p.m.

John Hill led the way when he opened his Broad Ripple Brewpub in 1990. Then Kwang Casey, inspired by Hill, opened Oaken Barrel in 1994 just south of town in Greenwood, Indiana.

Next was Alcatraz Brewing in 1995. It was a California-based company inspired by the infamous prison on Alcatraz Island near San Francisco Bay. It was the first downtown Indianapolis brewpub. It opened in the Circle Center Mall at the corner of Maryland and Illinois Streets. Guests entering from the street walked underneath a mock Golden Gate Bridge topped by a massive silo filled with malt. Once inside, the bright-red bridge continued. It led guests through the restaurant and to the bar. Decorated with tongue-in-cheek prison-vibe motif, Alcatraz was a place one could go for "the best beer behind bars." Brewers included Omar Castrellon, Skip Duvall, Belinda Short and Keely Thomlinson. It had about six rotating beers on tap. One of its most popular brews was Weiss Guy, an American wheat beer with a twist of lemon. It earned a gold medal at the World Beer Cup and a silver at the Great American Beer Festival.

There was a spike in 1996. Four brewpubs opened in Indianapolis that year. Rock Bottom Restaurant and Brewery opened at 10 West Washington Street. Although it was a chain restaurant headquartered in Boulder, Colorado, it played a key role in fostering a sense of community around craft beer in Indianapolis. Under brewmaster Jerry Sutherlin, Rock Bottom won four silver medals at the Indiana Brewers' Cup for Circle City Light, Raccoon Red Ale, Olde Number Ten strong ale and Goat Topper Maibock, as well as a bronze for Strong Scottish Ale. It later opened another location in College Park on the Northside of Indianapolis.

Circle V Brewing Company was next. It was founded by local home brewers Mark Vojnovich (nicknamed "V"), Curt Grelle and his wife, Julie. They opened the brewpub near Castleton Square Mall at the northwest corner of Eighty-Second and Craig Streets. Being one of a few independent, locally owned brewpubs in Indianapolis, it encouraged beer drinkers to take a break from chain restaurants and franchise brewpubs. "Bold Beer—Fresh Food—Hoosier Hospitality" was its slogan. It was known for its seasonal menu and wood-fired pizza—at a time when the farm-to-table movement was just beginning to take shape in Indianapolis and wood-fired pizzas were becoming a trend. It also hosted events and donated proceeds to local nonprofits. This is where Dave Colt of Sun King got his start. Circle V's popular Brickyard Red Ale boasted a good balance of malts and hops. Other beers included the Venus Blonde Ale, Probate Porter and Bullseye Bitter. In April 1999, it closed the restaurant and bar to focus solely on producing beer. It distributed beyond local boarders to places like Milwaukee, Louisville and Pennsylvania and produced about 650 barrels of beer a year.

There was also Glacier's End Brewing inside the Castleton Mall and Wildcat Brewing on north Michigan Road. Jeff Eaton founded Barley Island Brewing Company in historic downtown Noblesville in 1999. Ram Restaurant & [Big Horn] Brewery came next, a brewpub chain based in Lakewood, Washington. It opened in 2000 on Illinois Street in downtown Indianapolis, occupying the space of a former Planet Hollywood. After Circle V closed in 2001, Dave Colt began brewing at the Ram. He later brewed alongside assistant brewer, Clay Robinson, before they started Sun King together.

One of the last Indy brewpubs to open in the wake was Brugge Brasserie in 2005. Founded by internationally recognized brewmaster Ted Miller, it was the first gastropub in Indianapolis. This high-end pub in Broad Ripple specialized in Belgian-style fare and ales. It was most noted for its moules-frites and Triple de Ripple. Upland Brewing of Bloomington, Indiana, extended to South Broad Ripple by opening a tasting room in 2009 on College Avenue.

The brewpubs chugged steadily along, pairing great food with locally crafted brews. It was a new world of handcrafted ales. Quaffers began to discover beer tastes better fresh, straight from brewery to tap.

While the modern-day Indianapolis Brewing Company was a microbrewery that took an alternative approach to the "yellow fizzy stuff," it was operating on an old business model but on a "micro" scale. Some may argue that it lacked the heart and soul of craft. Because it was the first, old temperance-era laws prevented it from selling on-site and thus prevented it from having a taproom or opening a brewpub. It was wholesale only. It wasn't a destination spot. There was no sense of community—no gathering together at the brewery to share a few pints. It was strictly a production facility.

The first person to usher Indiana's craft beer movement (and who figured a clever way around the law) was John Hill. The on-site brewery at his Broad Ripple Brewpub in Indianapolis receives credit as the first craft brewery. Many followed suit. Then along came Sun King in 2009, the first to bring the modern concept of the production craft brewery to Indianapolis. In breaking away from the prevalent brewpub scene, it was the first in Indianapolis to dedicate its efforts entirely to beer and opened its brewery to visitors with an on-site tasting room where guests could drink beer fresh from the taps. It self-distributed, sold directly to the public, became the first craft brewery in Indiana to can its beer, focused strictly on the local market and, most importantly, created a space for community.

LESSONS IN SUN TEA

Ron Smith stood in front of the chilled florescent glow, surveying the selection of imports at the liquor store. His college days filled with parties and cases of cheap beer were coming to an end. Desiring something beyond the yellow fizzy stuff, he found his interests filtering toward more flavorful, specialty brews.

Settling in at home, he cracked open a bottle and grabbed a copy of the Sunday paper. The year was 1987. His eyes opened wide to an article in the *Indianapolis Star*. His gaze curiously fixed on a photograph of a guy with all sorts of bottles, hoses and tubes. The article featured a story on Paul Edwards talking about a small group of aficionados making homebrewed beer and that Joan Easley of Easley Winery had the ingredients and supplies. "I'd never really known anybody who homebrewed," explained Ron. "I don't think I even knew you could do such a thing. I was like, 'Holy cow…I need a hobby and that's it!'"

The next day, Ron made a trip to Indy's first homebrew supply shop. Actually, it was more like a little walk-in closet than a shop, as Ron described, since its focus was mainly wine. He grabbed a can of malt extract, some English hops, an old packet of Red Star–branded yeast and an index card with instructions and returned home to brew his first batch of homemade beer. Ron chuckled as he reminisced:

> *Back in those days the ingredients were awful. The yeast was like a step above bread yeast. These cans of extract were old…because in the beginning everything was from England and took a while to get. We made pretty good English ales but…it was very crude and we didn't know what we were doing.*
>
> *I made that first horrible batch of homebrew from Easley's, but it wasn't their fault. I set it out in the sun, I thought it was like sun tea (a trend in those days). I literally had no idea. It was in this big glass carboy and nobody said, "Don't put it in the sunlight." Nobody said that. And I had it sitting with the sun beating on it. For some reason, I thought it kind of looked like iced tea…so I thought…it's probably good for it. I had no idea it was going to skunk my beer. So my amber ale smelled like a skunk. It was phenolic and medicinal too…it smelled like Chloraseptic weed.*

Before the days of home internet, smartphones and endless amounts of information available at our fingertips, Paul Edwards, considered "Indianapolis's Grandfather of Homebrewing," helped found a small homebrewers club. They met one Sunday a month at the Broad Ripple Brewpub to try one another's brews, talk shop and refine their skills. The club always met after hours when the brewpub, by law, had to be closed on Sundays. The owner, John Hill, joined them. In 1998, the Hoosiers Organized to Produce Suds (HOPS) became known as the Foam Blowers of Indiana (FBI). As Ron described:

> *In those early years, the very first meeting I went to, I took some of that first batch and these guys would pull no punches. "Dude, that's bad!"…*

Ron Smith with homebrew equipment, circa 2005. *Ron Smith.*

but we'd dive into it. "What'd you do to make such bad beer?" And we'd
fix it. Some people were really proud and didn't want it torn down. So we
had a lot of one-timers. But the ones who came back [said], *"I'm going to*
make this better and show you." Almost every meeting we'd do evaluations,
and Paul Edwards was always teaching on judging beer.

Clubs like this formed not just in Indianapolis, but all over the nation. President Jimmy Carter made homebrewing legal on a federal level in 1978, fully ratified in February of the following year. The floodgates opened to a burst of homebrewing hobbyists. Interest followed curiosity to this idea of what beer could be.

People began researching and experimenting with recipes, drawing inspiration from the pale ales and brown beers of England as well as other European styles. They wrote books, formed clubs, held conferences and shared and expanded on one another's knowledge. Many of today's professional brewers have roots in homebrewing.

In 1995, Anita Johnson and her husband, Jim, purchased a dedicated homebrew supply shop called Great Fermentations and built it into a

Left: Indianapolis Brewing Company poster. *Indiana Historical Society, P0552.*

Below: Schmidt's Brewery poster. *Indiana Historical Society, P0552.*

Sign for Duesseldorfer at Washington and Illinois Streets, Indianapolis, Indiana, circa 1912. *Indiana Album, the Harley Sheets Collection.*

Left: Gold Medal Bock label. Indianapolis Brewing Company. *The Millers of Greenfield, Indiana.*

Right: Home Brewing Company tray. *The Millers of Greenfield, Indiana.*

Indianapolis Brewing Company beer cans: IBC Select, Gold Medal Lager and Progress. Circa 1930–1940s. *The Millers of Greenfield, Indiana.*

Indianapolis Brewing Company Duesseldorfer sign. *The Millers of Greenfield, Indiana.*

Left: Lieber Lager bar signage, circa 1930s. *The Millers of Greenfield, Indiana.*

Above: Lieber's Gold Medal Beer tip tray. *Dave Worthington Collection.*

Below: Painting of Capital City Brewing's "Taste Tells." *The Millers of Greenfield, Indiana.*

24th Annual Indiana Microbrewers Festival. *Brewers of Indiana Guild.*

Rita Kohn at Winterfest 2018. *Brewers of Indiana Guild.*

Above: Sandy Cockerham, Grand Master VIII (at time of publication), judging at the Aro Rojo competition. Mexico, 2019. *Sandy Cockerham.*

Left: ESB and Scottish eggs at Broad Ripple Brewpub. *Amy Beers.*

Indiana Amber from Oaken Barrel. *Amy Beers.*

Razz-Wheat from Oaken Barrel. *Amy Beers.*

Top: Oaken Barrel Brewpub before renovation. *Do317*.

Bottom: Oaken Barrel Brewpub, 2021. *Amy Beers*.

Clay Robinson (*left*) and Dave Colt (*right*) at Sun King Brewing. *Amy Beers.*

Sun King's patio. *Amy Beers.*

Left: Sun King's original house beers. *Amy Beers.*

Below: Eilise Lane of Scarlet Lane Brewing adds hops to the kettle, 2020. *Current Publishing, LLC. All Rights Reserved. Reprinted by permission.*

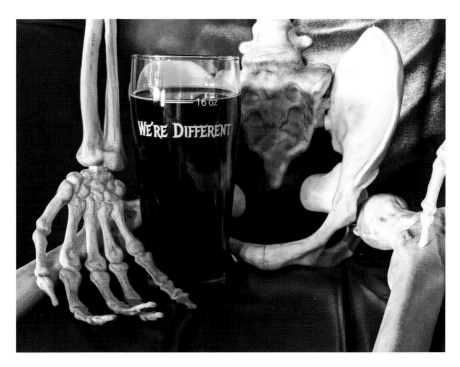

Scarlet Lane's Skelly poses with Dorian Stout. *Amy Beers.*

Dorian artwork at Scarlet Lane's Broad Ripple Taproom. *Kate Pantle.*

Home Brewing Company bottles at Indiana City Brewery. *Amy Beers.*

Indiana City Brewery. *Amy Beers.*

From left to right: Ryan, Jerry and Darren Conner inside the Bier Brewery taproom. *Amy Beers.*

Dan Krzywicki at Chilly Water. *Amy Beers.*

Eddie Sahm, 2021. *Carl Krockenberger*.

Oktoberfest at Half Liter, 2021. *Carl Krockenberger*.

Fountain Square Brewery. *Amy Beers*.

Left: Holly Miller of Black Acre Brewing with Saucy Intruder. *Holly Miller*.

Right: Leah and Nathan Huelsebusch of Taxman Brewery. *Taxman Brewing*.

Metazoa wins Brewery of the Year, 2021. *From left to right*: Grace Burns, Terra Courtney, Dale Van Deraa, Rob Malad and Nick Betzner. *Metazoa Brewing.*

St. Joseph Brewery. *Dauss Miller.*

From left to right: FBI founding members Paul Edwards, Tom Stilabower and Ron Smith. *Ron Smith.*

successful business. For a time, it was conveniently located across from the brewpub where the FBI met. Anita played an integral part in shaping the local beer community. Many lovingly refer to her as the "Mother of Indy's Craft Beer Scene." As a homebrewer herself, she taught classes. Brewers and beer aficionados alike would meet at the shop regularly just to talk beer. It became like a family. Some homebrewers worked at the shop before launching careers in professional brewing or starting their own breweries.

Darren Connor, for example, worked as the in-house brewer at the shop for ten years. During this time, he developed his now-famous recipe for PDG ("Pretty Darn Good") pale ale. In 2010, he opened Bier Brewery, just a few doors down on East Sixty-Fifth Street.

Shawn Kessel also worked at the shop before moving on to work at Grand Junction Brewery and then Taxman Brewing Company. Mark Havens, who later became a lead brewer at Daredevil, and Andrew Castner, who currently owns MashCraft Brewing, both worked at the shop for a time. Dan Krzywicki, another talented brewer, got his start working at Great Fermentations. He learned to homebrew and climbed the ladder to brew

Anita Johnson. *The Johnsons / Great Fermentations.*

professionally at Fountain Square Brewery. He is now head brewer and co-owner at Chilly Water Brewing Company. There were many others. Notably, Tonya Cornett was a frequent customer and avid homebrewer. Recognized internationally, she is now a professional brewer and an icon in the brewing industry.

Homebrewing served as the impetus of the craft beer movement. Anita's elevation of brewers was a major contributing factor in Indiana. Another significant impact came from her help in changing the state's homebrew laws. One of those laws prevented homebrewers from taking their brews outside the home, making the growth of craft beer a challenge. It was a hobby contained in a tiny box, just waiting for room to breathe. "The question back then was, 'Is homebrewing legal?' *And* 'Is it any good?'" explained Anita, "You can't answer 'Is it any good,' truthfully, if you can't give them a sample. So that was really important to us."

As fortune would have it, an intern at the statehouse, who happened to be a brewer, made contact with state representative Brian Hasler. So Anita—together with Paul Edwards, Steve Jackson, Jim Johnson and Julie Grelle—with the help of Hasler, changed the law. It took three years and was enacted on July 1, 1999. "[The craft beer renaissance in Indiana] started with homebrewers," described Anita, "but then you really needed to have a homebrew community to embrace the commercial craft beers because most consumers back then didn't really know about craft beer. They were used to Bud, Miller and Coors. The palate hadn't been created yet. These homebrewers were kind of these ale evangelists. We went to restaurants and demanded better beer. And everything grew."

When the Indiana law changed, it opened a new world of possibilities. It pulled homebrewing out of the box. A free-flowing exchange of homebrews and evangelical word-of-mouth provided a foundation for a developing industry. Microbrew festivals helped raise even more awareness.

As the industry grew, competitions fueled progress and innovation. The state fair had a prestigious, internationally renowned annual wine competition for both amateurs and professionals. After the homebrew law changed, it opened the doors for a beer competition. The Indiana State Fair Brewers' Cup was established in 1999 by fair board member Linda Moreau and Circle V's Julie Grelle. Anita Johnson later took over and further developed the program. Today, the Brewers' Cup continues as one of the most prestigious beer competitions. It consists of both homebrew and professional divisions.

In the beginning, the new Indiana Brewers' Cup gained a lot of media attention. It was very unique for its time. Subsequently, it drew more people

Winterfest 2018. *Brewers of Indiana Guild.*

into the hobby and fostered a sense of community. Competition also created a desire for education as brewers strove to advance their skills. They wanted to make the best product.

At first, they selected judges based solely on experience and knowledge. Then selection came by implementation of the Beer Judge Certification Program (BJCP). Paul Edwards pioneered teaching the technical aspects and evaluation of beer in Indianapolis. He, along with FBI member Tom Stilabower and Bill Friday, were some of the firsts in Indiana to officially become certified through the program.

I remember first meeting Tom at Great Fermentations during my studies for the Cicerone exam. I met up with Lindsay Jo, the second female Cicerone in Indiana who currently leads a local women beer professionals group and is the culinary arts operations manager at Newfields, to gather study materials at the shop. Tom spent nearly the whole day with us, making little individual baggies of malt and hop samples so we could train our palates. He answered endless amounts of questions.

Bill Friday (aka "The Button Guy") was an avid homebrewer from West Lafayette and ran the Tippecanoe Homebrewers Club. He made and sold buttons to help raise money for the club. He traveled extensively to beer events, spreading the word and making connections. He was well loved by many.

Anita Johnson described him in Rita Kohn's book *True Brew*: "The best way to describe Bill Friday is like a hummingbird. He was nowhere, and he was everywhere…he would be at homebrew club meetings all over the state. He would show up at beer tastings; he would show up at your house. He was like a hummingbird in that he would pollinate and carry things all over and spread it all around.…Everywhere he went, he promoted good beer."

After Bill passed, the Brewers' Cup created the Bill Friday Homebrew Club Award in his honor.

The Foam Blowers had a very technical beginning. This helped Ron Smith develop his skills and knowledge over the course of many years, as he recounted amusingly:

> *As the Brewers' Cup got bigger* [and brought in more judges], *some folks like me got frustrated.…I'm the low guy on the totem pole because I hadn't taken the test yet. I got some guy telling me I don't know what I'm talking about because he's BJCP judge and I'm not…and if I know so much…why don't I take the damn test.…Well, fine, I guess I better take the stupid test!*

Finally, in 2005, Ron decided to take the test. He also decided to lead a study group. "If I'm going to do this…I'm dragging a bunch of you assholes with me," he said playfully. The first session went well. Ron continued leading annual beer study groups and administered exams to help build the judge pool. "The more we created judges, the more we lifted up the whole community."

Just like Anita's homebrew classes at Great Fermentations, Ron Smith's BJCP classes developed many of today's beer professionals. Some of his first sessions included Jeff Eaton of Barley Island, Jon Lang of Triton and Sandy Cockerham, who is now a Grand Master VIII judge.

Ron had moved from novice homebrewer to judge to teacher. He won Best of Show at the first Brewers' Cup and later a Gold Medal at the National Homebrew Competition. He even had a beer release in 2006. Ron Smith's Castle Rock Irish Red Ale distributed to select stores throughout Indiana. He'd come a long way from his Chloraseptic sun tea beer:

> *I remember looking around a few years ago at the Brewers' Cup. I started counting. Almost half the people in the room, at the time, had been through my classes. Pro-brewers, homebrewers, BJCP judges…*

Foam Blowers of Indiana (FBI) win Homebrew Club of the Year. Tom Wallbank (*center*) poses with the Indiana Homebrewer of the Year award, surrounded by fellow club members and award winners, 2016. *Indiana State Fairgrounds & Event Center.*

ultimately, everybody's making better beer and next thing you know we have a whole community and a whole State that's becoming known for its beer. I mean, little Indiana has done pretty well....It's crazy...you've got the [unofficial] Sun King Rule at the Great American Beer Festival. They won too many [awards] and so the GABF changed it the next year so that you could only enter so many beers. They totally dominated. We've done some good things here in Indiana.

THE RIPPLE EFFECT

As if it were his own bloodshot eyes staring back at him, bleary-eyed John Hill focused intensely ahead at the two red taillights leading the way through a vast, disorienting blanket of white. His hands grew stiff, gripped tightly to the steering wheel. His heart thumped heavy in his chest. He hugged the ragged edge of the snow-drenched Rockies. His friends slept soundly inside the car. No snow tires. No chains. With little driving experience, his guiding force was the large truck ahead.

"If it went over the edge, I was going with it," jested John in his North Yorkshire accent over a proper pint of Extra Special Bitter at his cozy English-inspired pub. "A twenty-ounce pint is a *real* pint by the way," he added matter-of-factly.

The winter of 1967, he and his friends left for Indianapolis from Vancouver, Canada. Twenty-two-year-old John had just returned from finishing a contract in Toronto. He was working as an electrician in the copper mines but wasn't doing anything at the time. He had settled in for a pint at the local neighborhood pub in Vancouver when his friends showed up.

"We're leaving," they said.

"Where are you going?" asked John.

"Indianapolis."

"Do you have any room?" And with that, he threw his bags in, jumped in the car and went. "If you're in your twenties or thirties and you get an opportunity, just go for it. At some point when you get older, you'll have to settle down, look to the future and what you're going to do for retirement. But when you're young and if it doesn't work out, you still have time to start over," offered John with his grandfather-like wisdom.

John is now living his retirement dream. He built the Broad Ripple Brewpub to emulate his hometown pub in North Yorkshire. "Where I come from, we have some of the best beer in the country. All I wanted was a place like in England where I could go outside and talk to all my friends and drink beer," he explained. Little did he know, as he followed his youthful whims during that February blizzard, that he would venture to make history for Indiana's craft beer scene.

John arrived in Indianapolis that winter to discover a beer desert. Options were slim. Then Shallo's Antique Restaurant and Brewhaus opened in 1981, followed by the Ale Emporium in 1982. They started offering imports to accommodate a growing trend toward specialty brews. Demand for something beyond the standard domestic lager began to increase.

John was ready to retire from construction. He had little interest in learning to brew. "I didn't know anything about brewing beer—just what it tasted like," he said cheekily. He had no desire to open a commercial brewery for distribution or a bar that offered imports. He didn't care about growing a large moneymaking business. "You need money to get through life, but it was more about having a good time and doing something peopled enjoyed,' he explained. "Stuff in the bottle isn't as good as a fresh beer. You can't beat that."

Craft beer was on the rise. John traveled to the California breweries for inspiration. Like Peters and Harris of the Indianapolis Brewing Company, he also paid a visit to Jamie Emerson at Hood River Brewing in Oregon—not to learn brewing, but rather to understand the facility and how it operated. From his research, he compiled an estimate to have a brewpub built from scratch. He learned that was too expensive, so he decided to build it himself.

One day, he drove past the Broad Ripple Auto Parts store. He noticed a man unloading car parts. He drove around the block and struck up a conversation. The man had been trying to lease the space. John told him his plans for a brewpub. They struck a deal; John would lease the building for five dollars per square foot. At the end of their twenty-year term, he promised to buy the building.

The auto parts store was a plain cinder block building. Drawing on his knowledge of construction, John added walls, stained glass, dark wood paneling, a decorative tin ceiling, the bar and a fireplace. With help from his Hoosier-born wife, Nancy, they transformed the space into a cozy English-style pub. In 1990, the Broad Ripple Brewpub opened on East Sixty-Fifth Street. It's nestled close to the Monon Trail, a railway turned pedestrian pathway. It was the first brewpub in Indiana.

When he opened, that pesky temperance-era law was still in place. One could not own a retail license *and* a brewing license. Beer could not be sold on the same site it was brewed. This made operating a brewpub somewhat

The Broad Ripple Brewpub. *Amy Beers.*

complicated. So, what did John do? He thought outside the box, found a loophole. He created a corporation that owned the building. Nancy rented the restaurant and John the brewery.

A wall stood between the brewing tanks and the restaurant. There was no door between them. Two separate buildings. Clever. "I had to get a letter from the Feds so we could transfer the beer," explained John. They put a hole through the wall. This allowed them to serve beer straight from the serving tanks. When it was time to fill an order, they stuck a non-permanent pipe through the wall and delivered the beer through the pipe. Then they pulled the pipe back. Technically, it wasn't connected. A sign hung on the tank in the brewery. It read "Property of Broad Ripple Brewing Company" on one side. The other side read, "Property of Broad Ripple Brewpub." They would flip the sign accordingly. Today, they still serve beer directly from the serving tanks, except that pesky law changed in 1993, so the process isn't so complicated.

John and his Broad Ripple Brewpub played key influence to Indiana's booming craft beer scene. Like a pebble dropped into a pond, it created a ripple effect. (When I mentioned this during our interview, John dryly responded, "Well we *are* in Broad Ripple"…and then requested he be paid royalties if I used the pun in the book.)

Although he doesn't like the attention (and just wants to drink his beer), John is often lovingly referred to as the "Mayor of Broad Ripple," "Lord Hill" and the "Father of Indiana's Craft Beer Scene." During the brewpub's thirtieth anniversary celebration, the community honored John with an Indiana State Brewers' Cup Golden Growler Award, which he humbly accepted. It's no wonder the accolades are frequent. His brewpub served as an incubator, forging a path that helped foster curiosity, progress knowledge and inspire and develop early talent.

Before the brewpub, he and Nancy owned the Corner Wine Bar. They worked with a distributor to curate imports sourced from Chicago. They hosted tastings and introduced local beer drinkers to ales like Duval from Belgium. Slowly, palates developed for beer outside the standard American lager.

When the brewpub opened, John hosted the Foam Blowers of Indiana homebrew club. In 1996, he helped organize the first Indiana Microbrewer's Festival with his brewer at the time, Kevin Matalucci. "One year we made a bubble gum beer for the festival, and it went like crazy," recalled John. "People asked how we made it, 'How did you get that bubble gum flavor?' We told them, 'Well we just sat in the back and we chewed bubble gum and spit it into the keg.'…But just for the record, we did use flavoring."

Several Indiana brewers began their careers at the Broad Ripple Brewpub. With full support from John, they later started breweries of their own. Greg Emig was one of the first brewers for the brewpub. In 1993, he opened Lafayette Brewing Company. It is the second-oldest continually operating brewery in Indiana. Then there was Ted Miller, who opened the Belgian-inspired Brugge Brasserie within walking distance from the brewpub. Kevin Matalucci worked at the brewpub for nearly two decades. He moved up the ranks to head brewer when Ted's position became available. Kevin now owns Twenty Tap in South Broad Ripple. It offers local and regional craft beers, as well as its house beers, brewed downstairs at Twenty Below Brewing. John Treeter studied under Kevin. He eventually became brewmaster at Greenwood's Oaken Barrel. Originally from Union Brewing Company, followed by the former Flat 12 Brewery, Jonathon Mullens is now brewer at the Broad Ripple Brewpub.

Experience visiting the brewpub inspired Kwang Casey to open his own brewpub. In 1994, he founded the Oaken Barrel Brewing Company with partners Bill Fulton and founding head brewer Brook Belli. It was the second craft brewery of the Greater Indianapolis region. From this

From left to right: Greg Emig, John Hill, Gil Alberding, Kevin Matalucci and Ted Miller at Broad Ripple Brewpub's 20th Anniversary Celebration, 2010. *Broad Ripple Brewpub.*

brewpub sprang a whole new web of Indy beer professionals who later branched out to other breweries.

Jerry Sutherlin worked at Oaken Barrel a year after it opened. He got his start waiting tables, bartending, making deliveries and handling kegs and then, eventually, brewing. He's since been noted as one of the "uncles" of Indiana's craft beer scene, having mentored a new generation of brewers and serving as an anchor for the downtown brewpubs. After Oaken Barrel, he worked for a short time alongside Dave Colt at the Ram Restaurant & Brewery before becoming brewmaster at Rock Bottom downtown. He brewed there for more than a decade. In 2016, he opened his own brewery alongside co-owners Eric Fear and Max Schenk. Round Town Brewery was located near the White River, fortuitously within a mile of Indy's first brewery, Wernweg & Young. Jerry currently works downtown at Goodwood Brewing, in the former Ram location.

Others from Oaken Barrel include Mark Havens, who became head brewer at Big Woods Brewing Company and Quaff ON! and, later, Daredevil Brewing. Andrew Castner got his start at Oaken Barrel in 2006, studying under Havens, and then became head brewer at the Ram before opening MashCraft in 2014. Then there is Alan Simons, now head brewer at St. Joseph Brewery. Tonya Cornett, who is currently brewing in Oregon,

Darren Connor of Bier Brewery and Scott Ellis of Big Lug all brewed at Oaken Barrel for a short while before ending up at their current breweries.

Inspired by Oaken Barrel, Mad Anthony Brewing Company opened in Fort Wayne, Indiana, in 1998. In addition to helping Oaken Barrel, John also helped Mad Anthony and Mishawaka Brewing get established through his consulting work. One brewery begat another brewery, which begat another, until Indiana's beer scene became what it is today.

In 2000, John Hill helped organize the Brewers of Indiana Guild and served as its first president. The guild is a nonprofit trade association that provides a unifying voice for the craft breweries and brewpubs of Indiana. It works to promote awareness and appreciation for the award-winning talent and variety of beers produced in Indiana, support local brewers through annual conferences and regional meetings that provide educational and networking opportunities and advocate for favorable regulatory treatment from state and federal agencies. "Everyone was getting accolades on the East and West Coasts, and Indiana had great beer," explained John. "There were about a half dozen of us at the time in Indiana. So I started the guild to get the word out about Indiana…and for camaraderie and to help each other out. It's a great business."

In the first decade of Indiana's budding craft beer scene, many early brewers won awards from some of the most prestigious brewing competitions. The Extra Special Bitter from Broad Ripple Brewpub was the first from Indiana to receive an award at the Great American Beer Festival. It took home a gold medal in 1991. Others to win awards at the GABF included Mishawaka Brewing, Oaken Barrel, Alcatraz, the Evansville Brewery and Mad Anthony's in Fort Wayne. Mishawaka Brewing and Mad Anthony's even went up against the big guys at the World Beer Cup and took home awards, and Alcatraz won several.

"We're still making the same beer we made thirty years ago," John modestly declared as we finished the last drops of our Extra Special Bitter. "I still love beer. When I go back home [to England], I still go to the same exact pub every time. It's not the beer—it's the camaraderie. It's not the product—it's the people. Meeting places are important. I created this place, but people have to come…otherwise it's nothing."

John could have played it safe and ordered another pint at that pub in Vancouver. And who knows where Indiana's craft beer scene would be today if it hadn't been for that truck's guiding light.

THIS ISN'T A SPORTS BAR

The soft glow of a seventeen-inch color television sat squarely in the corner of a dimly lit Broad Ripple Brewpub. The year was 1992. It was a good year for Indiana basketball. All eyes were on IU as Bobby Knight led the team to multiple victories. There was much excitement and sense of pride as some of the team's best players had played high school basketball in Indiana. The biggest win that season came when IU battled against the incomparable UCLA in a revenge win that sent them to the Final Four. On top of beating such a powerhouse team, IU scored in the triple digits. This was unheard of in college basketball, especially in an NCAA tournament.

Fans went crazy! It was must-see TV. Before the days of internet and smartphone technology, if you wanted to know real-time results, you had to watch the game live on television. It was common for family and friends to gather at sports bars to cheer on their team.

Kwang Casey and his friend sat together in front of the Broad Ripple Brewpub's television, cheering loudly as IU sank shot after shot. "Hey you've gotta keep it down," informed the staff. "This isn't a sports bar."

Kwang was a regular at the brewpub. And the staff at the brewpub were regulars at the Broad Ripple Steakhouse, a restaurant he managed just two blocks down the road. He worked in restaurants all through high school and college. He'd studied engineering but loved the hospitality industry. As manager, he helped build a successful steakhouse. After its ten o'clock closing time, the restaurant would turn into a neighborhood bar that catered to musicians and fellow industry people. "It kind of became an alternative punk-rock bar," explained Kwang. "It became very popular. So the guys from Broad Ripple Brewpub started coming. That's how I got interested in beer. I'd go over there and drink craft beer."

As the final seconds ticked off the clock, there was never a doubt that the local heroes had beaten the mighty Bruins. The buzzer sounded. Shouts and cheers turned to laughter and exuberance.

"You've gotta keep it down!" echoed in the quiet, cozy brewpub as the band on TV began playing the IU fight song.

"Not a sports bar?" said Kwang to himself, baffled. "But it's beer. I know it's craft beer…but why would you not mix the two together?" Then, jokingly, he said out loud, "You know what, I'm going to open a brewery. I'm going to put TVs everywhere! It's going to be kind of sports bar meets brewery." But the more he thought about it, he said, "You know….that's a good idea! I'm going to pursue it."

So Kwang pursued the idea with his good friend Bill Fulton. They grew up together in Greenwood. Bill lived in Atlanta at the time, where he ran into their mutual college friend Kristen, who also lived there. Bill became friends with her husband, Brook Belli. He was a homebrewer and introduced Bill to craft beer. They wanted to open a brewery in Atlanta, but the laws back then made it difficult. The laws in Indiana had just changed to where you could brew and serve on the premises. So, Kwang and Bill talked Brook into moving to Indianapolis and be head brewer at the brewery they wanted to open.

The trio formed a partnership. Each had backgrounds in engineering and a passion for craft beer. "Knowing engineering helps with the brewing process," said Fulton to the local paper. "Brewing is like a mini-engineering project."

It also helped that Kwang had restaurant and management experience, Bill had an MBA from Duke and Brook was a graduate from the prestigious Siebel Institute, a brewmaster school in Chicago. In 1994, on the Fourth of July weekend, they opened Oaken Barrel Brewpub at a strip mall location in Greenwood. "I'm a TV junkie," exclaimed Kwang. "I've got thirteen TVs at home. So I put TVs everywhere [inside the brewpub]. The timing was perfect. Sports was huge here all of the sudden. We had the crowd."

The Colts made the AFC Championship game in 1995. There was also the infamous, ongoing feud between the Pacers and the Knicks—a rivalry fueled by Reggie Miller. Back then, there weren't many restaurants with TVs in Kwang's neighborhood. It was a golden opportunity for Oaken Barrel to offer a casual sports atmosphere combined with great food and craft beer.

At first, Kwang wanted to focus on beer. The menu they offered fit on one piece of paper. It included five appetizers, five sandwiches and five entrées. The chef who worked with him at the steakhouse came down after he opened, took a look at the menu and said, "That's not going to work." He crumpled up the paper, tossed it into the trash and revamped the whole menu. From then on, they were a full-service restaurant. "He's a very creative chef," affirmed Kwang, "fantastic specials and menu ideas. So we became more restaurant than brewpub. The Southside was dying for some simple but good food at a casual atmosphere. From then on, we were running. People came for the beer out of curiosity but came back because of the food."

New businesses are risky, especially as a forerunner in a new craft beer industry. Oaken Barrel came with its own set of challenges. The main challenge was introducing patrons to craft beer and persuading them to drink it. Indiana was a little behind in the craft movement. Many thought it was just a fad and would soon disappear. It took years to catch on and cultivate interest, as Kwang explained:

> *It was challenging trying to educate people. I started matching beer with food, and people thought I was crazy. People were reluctant. But at the same time, we were the only ones. Interest piqued. People came from all over the state to try our beer, from Elkhart to Louisville. We had a group that would come up once a month on a bus. They'd go to the Broad Ripple Brewpub, then the ball game, then here. It was unique enough. It was an attraction.*
>
> *A lot of people didn't like hoppy beers. We had a blonde ale that was popular. Then we introduced a Belgian wit, and that was a big hit, and then a red ale. You could just see the guy who wouldn't drink any craft beer when we first opened…we had domestics in bottles (and still do)…but he became an avid craft beer drinker. And I just look back twenty-seven years ago, when he'd say, "Nope, you'll never get me to drink that stuff." Now he's a beer connoisseur.*

There was also the challenge of zoning, property tax and building permits—ensuring that everything was up to code. Brewpubs were so new, and Indiana was not set up to handle the legalities. There was a lack of resources and departments to handle a craft beer industry. The process leading up to opening day was slow-going and approvals delayed. "The fire department didn't know what a brew kettle was," began Kwang. "'How do we inspect this?' They showed up during construction but wouldn't give us permits. Then one day, one of the firemen who owned a local landscape company on the side was doing flowers here for the landlord. He saw the tanks and asked what they were. He found out they were beer tanks and got so excited. So he told everyone at the fire department about it, and then word got to the fire chief and inspectors. It sped things up for us to get approved. Now, half of the mug club is the fire department."

Family and friends kept them afloat the first few years. Kwang figured that, in the worst-case scenario, if the beer side didn't work, he knew he could run a successful restaurant. But the beer side *did* experience success. Oaken Barrel burst at the seams after only a year and a half in business. What started as a five-thousand-square-foot restaurant with a brewery grew to include an additional four-hundred-square-foot banquet room and a six-hundred-square-foot brewhouse bar. With extra room in the brewing area and plans to start bottling, they expected to triple production. In 1997, they expanded into a dedicated production facility for distribution.

Kwang's partner, Bill, had dreams of becoming a regional brewery. Although the three entrepreneurs hadn't planned on growing so fast, it happened that the guys from the Indianapolis Brewing Company were on their way out—perfect timing for the brewpub. Oaken Barrel bought the IBC's warehouse and equipment, making it Indiana's largest microbrewery.

Oaken Barrel already distributed to draft lines at more than two dozen local restaurants across the Greater Indianapolis region and did contract brewing for Scotty's Brewhouse. Beers included Meridian Street Lager, Snake Pit Porter, Gnaw Bone Pale Ale, Victory Amber and Razz-Wheat Ale. It had just started bottling, but the lack of space at the brewpub in Greenwood stunted its growth—capped at two thousand barrels per year. The warehouse created room for a ten-thousand-barrel capacity. There was the production brewery in the former IBC facility for distribution only, and the brewpub brewery continued brewing for the restaurant.

Shortly after, a sales manager at Monarch Beverage visited the brewpub to try its Razz-Wheat. Brook had been brewing its raspberry wheat ale from the beginning as a seasonal summer beer. It won a silver medal at the Great American Beer Festival in 1995, just a year after it opened. His secret weapon? He used real raspberry purée instead of extract. It was so popular that they decided to make it a regular house beer. Subsequently, Razz-Wheat developed a cult following. For a time, it was Indiana's top-selling brewpub beer. Even today, Razz-Wheat is the quintessence of Oaken Barrel.

Thanks to Razz-Wheat, Oaken Barrel got its foot in the door with Monarch Beverage, which began distributing its beer. Then Victory Field opened in 1996. Shortly after, Razz-Wheat became available at the ballpark along with Victory Amber, brewed specifically for Victory Field. Oaken Barrel had also purchased rights to the IBC's beer and labels. This amber ale included a remake of an Indianapolis Brewing Company label. It featured "Victory Girl," inspired by Monument Circle's Lady Victory.

Bill was thrilled by the Victory Field contract. As much as he loved craft beer, he was an even bigger fan of baseball. Soon the Indianapolis Indians offered him a job he couldn't refuse. He left the brewpub for five years. When he returned, he felt out of place. Some people didn't even know who he was. As Kwang divulged:

> *We had someone interested in buying…it was a low-ball offer. So Bill looked at me and said, "This was your vision, and I'm glad I helped make it happen. I'll sell you my share for half price." So I bought him out. My lease was up at the IBC. I got out of that, sold the equipment,*

Kwang Casey at Oaken Barrel. *Amy Beers.*

recouped my money. This was in 2004. Then we expanded over here [at the brewpub]. I decided to streamline and not go after the distribution market. West Coast and East Coast beer was starting to come here, so it was more competitive. I saw the writing on the wall. We'd made enough noise, especially after Sun King opened. We'd attracted the attention of these other breweries from the coasts. We'd become a beer town.

Kwang attributes the brewpub's success to advice his grandfather gave, support from his wife, his loyal customers and community who've kept him in business (especially during the COVID pandemic) and his staff, many of whom have been with him since opening day:

The service is top-notch. People appreciate that more than anything. Donna came two months after we opened, and she's been here for twenty-seven years. She's awesome…my best waitress. I joke, "I spend more time with you than with my wife." And she yells at me more than my wife! But she also guides me because some things I just don't see. She stays on top of things. My chefs have been here since the steakhouse. One of the chefs, we used to work together when we were teenagers. The kitchen manager has been here twenty-six years and started as a dishwasher—the cold kitchen

144

manager for twenty-five years, since he was a kid. My grandfather gave me good advice when I first opened: "Treat your staff like family and customers like guests in your house." That was good advice.

Kwang moved to the United States from South Korea when he was thirteen years old. His biological father passed away when he was three years of age. His mother passed as they were making plans for his emigration so he could attend school in America. His aunt and uncle who lived in Indianapolis decided to adopt him:

I call them my parents. They raised me. They're both Korean but only spoke English around me so I'd learn more quickly. I grew up with American culture. When I was sixteen I had a hot rod…racing up and down the strip. I went to college here and met my wife. She's American.

My parents taught me good work ethic. My mom made me get a paper route when I first came to America. My dad would wake up Sunday morning at 4:30 with his Chevy Blazer. I'm sure he didn't want to do that. But he did it so I would learn the value of a dollar.

It seems that Kwang's hard work has paid off. "I've had offers of people wanting to buy, but I don't want to retire because I enjoy it. I look forward to coming to work every day." Oaken Barrel still boasts an abundance of televisions because it is, in fact, a sports bar. The first craft beer sports bar in Indiana.

A MODERN-DAY CRAFT BEER SCENE, 2009-2022

THE KINGS OF CRAFT

The sharp, pungent, vinegar-like odor of acetic acid filled the cramped 1,200-square-foot brewery crammed with kegs and equipment. The air was dense with steam. Thick, with the lingering scent of spent grain. Dave Colt and Clay Robinson scrubbed the floor. They polished the copper on the tanks until it sparkled. It was quiet. The Ram Restaurant & Brewery closed for its monthly two-day, floor-to-ceiling deep clean. Dave and Clay neared the end of their ten-hour shift. A gasket, loosened for cleaning, let out a big, tired sigh.

Clay squeezed through the top opening of the mash tun for a breath. He made eye contact with Dave, who'd just finished sterilizing a beer hose. "What would you do if you could open your own brewery?" asked Clay, as if to extract and solidify the mutual thoughts of the moment.

The duo spent time reflecting on their decade-long experiences in the brewing industry. The best and the worst, their experiences working with other people, what they liked and didn't like. How they would do it differently, that is, *if* they were to open their own brewpub. "What drives you crazy about this place?" led to more serious topics like, "What culture would we want to inspire, how would we treat our employees, how would we give back to the community." And finally, there was the big question: "Should we do this?"

What began as a distraction from an unfulfilling gig at a corporate brewpub chain turned into a three-year-long conversation, which eventually led to the creation of an Indianapolis brewing empire.

Before they became the kings of Indy's craft beer scene, Dave and Clay worked their way up the ranks. In the late 1990s, Dave worked as a bartender, bar manager and assistant brewer at the now-defunct Circle V Brewing Company. Clay was fresh out of college. He was working at Roscoe's Tacos in Greenwood. The two met for the first time when Clay was on his way to a Phish concert in Noblesville. He stopped at the Circle V to pick up some beer. Dave helped load a keg into the back of Clay's Volkswagen Westfalia, and the two went their separate ways. They would not meet again until years later.

Dave became the head brewer at the Ram downtown. Meanwhile, Clay quit the taco joint. He became a server at Rock Bottom Restaurant and Brewery, also located downtown. He worked his way to assistant brewer and, finally, head brewer.

The craft beer community in Indianapolis was small in the early 2000s. So, when destiny brought Dave and Clay back together, it was one of those, "Hey…I think I know you" moments. The two became fast friends and met regularly to talk shop.

Clay became increasingly dissatisfied working under a corporate culture. He calls it his "Angry Clay" period. His strong disinclination working for corporations was influenced by his father's experience. Omar, Clay's father, sold his food production company to a subsidiary of Anheuser-Busch in 1982 but stayed on as president. "He was increasingly bitter and upset about the corporate culture," explained Clay. "I watched my dad go through this thing when I was a kid, and it left a big impression on me. He just kept butting heads because he went from running a company that he'd helped build and made all of the decisions to having to do what other people said."

Clay quit the corporate grind at Rock Bottom. For the next few years, he traveled the country in limbo. He worked the odd construction job, hung out with friends and family and caught up on some reading until he used up all his savings.

In 2005, Dave offered Clay a job working with him at the Ram. Even though Clay despised working for corporations, he needed a source of income and didn't see many other options. It was back under the corporate thumb. "What would you do if you could open your own brewery?" became a resonating theme for the next three years. Clay explained: "Brewpubs were all we knew and it was all we had in Indianapolis. When we were planning, it was more like; this is what we know…we do this thing. It was increasingly unsatisfying, the more you dream up the thing you want to do, to go work for someone else every single day. We could be doing this for ourselves."

"Yes, we could be working much harder and longer hours…for a lot less money," quipped Dave, noting the experience that many young entrepreneurs face in the early days of a startup business.

Dave and Clay teamed with friends in the restaurant industry who also had dreams of their own. The original plan was for a brewpub focused on seasonality and local ingredients. They wanted a menu complete with beer and food pairings. The two were especially ready for the freedom to show their creative side with constantly rotating seasonal brews. However, challenges arose that would send the team in different directions.

Over the course of a year, the beer side and the food side couldn't reach an agreement on the structure of their business. Additionally, the search for affordable real estate conducive to the foot traffic needed to build a successful restaurant proved difficult. "Restaurants cost a lot of money to open and breweries cost a lot of money to open, and the two of them together cost twice as much money," explained Clay.

But they didn't give up. Dave and Clay met with the chef at his house. After several menu ideas and iterations, still, nothing was coming to fruition. They left. Standing in their friend's driveway, Clay looked at Dave, frustrated, and said, "We're not getting anywhere with this. I don't care about the restaurant, you don't care about the restaurant. We want to make beer. So what if we just make beer?"

Another "what if" followed. "I'm notoriously bad at math, and I'm not even really good at Excel," remarked Clay, "but I was doing our Excel spreadsheets at the time. And so I went in and I took out all the restaurant stuff like the salaries for restaurant staff and cost of goods. I came back to Dave the next day and was like, 'Look, it can work.'" Clay continued with more research. He dug through online brewpub reviews from all over the country and discovered a general theme. Customers raved about the beer more so than the food.

Another lightbulb moment for Clay was realizing that other major metropolitan cities across the country had production craft breweries. Iconic breweries like Stone Brewing in San Diego, the Great Divide in Denver and Brooklyn Brewing in New York had all become part of that city's identity. Indianapolis didn't have that. What followed was a really awkward breakup with their restaurant friends (who eventually got over it, opened a successful restaurant and even were one of the first to offer Sun King beer at their establishment). "It's like the brakes came off and the train went forward at a hundred miles per hour because at that point it was like, okay, boom," exclaimed Clay.

"The groundwork was being laid," added Dave, referencing the community's growing love and awareness for craft beer. "We were building a customer base, each one of us in the industry. That's all really. So we were standing on the shoulders of people who already got some laws changed to make it happen for the city. We were kind of like, we should be those people that take the next leap."

But first, they had to get funding…and probably find a building. That June, in 2008, Clay went all-in. He found his replacement at work and quit his job at the Ram. He took a break to focus on writing the business plan and spent the summer with his now-wife in her hometown in Alaska. They returned to Indy in September, and Clay was ready to follow his dream. Then the 2008 financial crisis hit, sending the world into the worst economic recession since the Great Depression.

"Do you really think it's a good idea to leave your job and start your own business?" Clay recalled in a conversation with his mother. "Are you kidding me?" he responded. "I already left my job! There's no going back now. It's only forward."

Dave learned of the crisis watching the news while vacuuming at home. He had three small children to consider, yet he remained optimistic: "The worst thing would be that the brewery doesn't work. I still had a job, a skill set, and I was employable." Although the timing wasn't perfect, they were already in too deep. The determined Indianapolis brewers pressed on toward their dream. "The economy took a huge stinking dump on everybody. We were leaving perfectly good jobs that were paying us. It was elation and vomit all at the same time."

Clay reached out to his father, Omar Robinson—who had more than fifty years' experience in food distribution, manufacturing and sales—to help revise and create the final business plan. They also had help from attorney Steve Koers, who was a big fan of Dave and Clay's beers. He worked in exchange for beer and put in some sweat equity as their business attorney for a small percentage of the company. Next entered Andy Fagg, the final piece of the puzzle.

Andy was a successful businessman and a regular at the Circle V back when Dave was bartending. The old friends had been discussing the brewery plans. When the plan was complete, Dave asked if Andy would give it a once over and poke holes in it. While Dave and Clay knew a lot about beer, they didn't know a lot about business. "More important than your strengths are your weaknesses," said Clay. "You need to find people who make up for that."

Dave was out of town at the Great American Beer Festival representing the Ram, so Clay and Omar met with Andy for lunch to go over the plan. Andy was a jovial guy. After a few beers and even more questions after reading over the plan, he set down his beer and said, "Well, I'm glad you're not doing the restaurant. Those are super risky. Also, what about the Hop Crisis?"

The hop shortage of 2008 was a real concern, leaving a huge dent in the craft beer industry. According to *Inc. Magazine*:

> *Fed up with habitually low prices, some farmers pulled out their hop vines and trellises to plant other crops, thus reducing the total acreage of hops in cultivation worldwide by roughly half. Key growing regions in the Czech Republic and Slovenia were hit by bad weather, further reducing the supply. Meanwhile, consumers were developing a taste for rich, aromatic beer…leading craft beer makers to use more hops in their recipes. Prices skyrocketed, and brokers began to run alarmingly low on inventory. The situation was particularly dire for small American brewers. Big producers and even most large regional players sign long-term contracts that provide them with an annual supply at a fixed price. Many craft brewers, on the other hand, buy hops as they go. Now, suddenly, there was nothing to buy.*

Luckily, Dave had already secured a contract with a hop supplier. "Wow. You guys really have your shit together," exclaimed Andy. "This is great. I'm in!" And with that, they all stood up and shook hands.

Clay hopped into the driver's seat of his car. He hung his hand over the ignition with a half-turn of the keys. He turned to his dad and said, a bit befuddled, "Did we just get funded?"

"I was excited but I don't think I really quite grasped it," recalled Clay. "You don't want to look a gift horse in the mouth. I didn't want to ask too many questions…like, 'Ok, you're in!? That's fantastic! I don't know whether it's for fifty bucks or one hundred grand. What does that mean?' But I'm just going to ride this high out, and I'm going to go home and feel really good about the fact that something is happening and we're getting some traction on our dreams."

Clay called Dave, who was still at the Great American Beer Festival, to share the news. Dave was over the moon. Plus, they had just won prestigious gold and silver medals for two of their barrel-aged beers. This confirmed in Andy's mind that he'd made the right decision. He came on as a partner. Not wanting to fund it all himself, he organized a group of investors. "We got the money in one day, but it was more challenging to find a building. I thought it'd be the other way around," exclaimed Clay. "It took six months and thirteen different buildings to land here at College Avenue."

They waited until they had funding and a building to start telling people about the brewery. "But how are you going to make any money if it's not a brewpub?" they would ask. "How are you going to get funded?" others would say. But they were already funded, and the train moved full speed ahead.

Sun King Brewing opened in July 2009—the first production craft brewery in Indianapolis. The name generated from the idea of seasonality and the governing sun responsible for the changing seasons. It self-distributed and offered a tasting room for patrons inside the brewery. Volunteers lined up to work the tap lines in the excitement of being part of the growing craft beer scene. In its first year, the goal was to produce one thousand barrels of beer— five thousand barrels within the first five years. It did five hundred barrels in the first six months and were on track to produce five thousand barrels that same year. "We joke around a lot," said Clay, "but we grossly underestimated the demand. Rapid growth is challenging. To continue quickly meeting demand while making sure quality is top, but also it was a lot of fun."

In 2011, just two years after opening, Sun King made history at the Great American Beer Festival in Boulder, Colorado. It won eight medals, including four gold. It was the most ever won by a single brewery at a single event in more than twenty-five years.

"The year before we'd won two medals," recalled Dave as he began to tell the story. "No one had really heard of us.…But in 2011, the craziest part is, we went down to collect our first medal, and Paul Gatza, the director of the Brewer's Association…"

"He's the guy with the clip board that says 'hi' and checks you off when you go get your medal," explained Clay.

"So he's looking down at his clipboard with his headset, very stern, and says, 'You guys might want to stick around,'" continued Dave. "I was like, 'Heck yeah man, we're going to party! We won a medal!' Then we get off stage and hear our name called again. And then I think by the eighth one it dawned on us, 'Ohhhh…*this* is what he was talking about.'"

"The eighth one was kind of the best one," added Clay, "because it was for Johan the Barleywine, which was the first batch of beer we ever brewed at Sun King."

There were eight Sun King representatives at the festival that year. Before they won the awards, someone from the group joked, "Hey, wouldn't it be hilarious if we each won a medal?"

"We were on stage for the medal we'd won previously, which was the seventh medal," Clay went on, "and as we were getting that medal, they read our name for the last medal for the last category."

"And it was the gold medal because it was the last medal of the ceremony," noted Dave.

"So we were on stage getting a medal when we get another medal," laughed Clay. "We were jumping up and down."

To celebrate, they each wore a medal to the Chop House for dinner, a place that normally requires reservations. But as they each walked in, one by one with their medals, the staff took congratulatory notice. "All of a sudden we were able to get a table," exclaimed Dave.

And then, of course, lots of beer drinking followed suit. "We were being kind of silly," continued Dave, recalling the night's events. "I felt so ecstatic. At one point it was like I couldn't feel my feet touching the floor. We each took turns wearing all of the medals at the same time."

Sweeping up the competition opened doors for the new kings of craft. Distributors from almost every state began knocking on their door. They had several good meetings in the weeks to follow but ultimately decided that they didn't want to stretch themselves too thin. They were already growing at a pace they could hardly keep up with. A meeting at the round table with their team ended with a firm conclusion: what they were already doing worked. They just wanted to continue selling beer in Indiana. "Trying to reach for the stars would ruin what we're doing and who we are," Clay said, "so let's just be Sun King. We don't need to borrow millions of dollars to chase millions of more dollars."

In 2010, just eight months after it opened, Sun King earned bragging rights as the first craft brewery in Indiana to can its beer. This made its product more accessible and widely available. It took off like wildfire. The following year, Sun King produced more than eighteen thousand barrels of beer, far exceeding its original goal of five thousand barrels in the first five years. In 2016, they invested a total of $4 million in expansion projects to make room for 240 fermentation tanks, update equipment and hire additional staff, which included about thirty-five full-time and fifty part-time employees.

House beers included (and still include) Sunlight Cream Ale, Osiris "Indiana" Pale Ale and Wee Mac Scottish-style ale. As their brand grew,

Sun King continued winning awards and gaining both local and national recognition. They signed contracts with Victory Field and Lucas Oil Stadium after fans continually asked for their beer during sporting events. They ran out of Sun King beer opening night at Lucas Oil before it was even halfway into the game because demand was so high.

Then Yuengling came to town and challenged local craft breweries. To navigate a changing marketplace, Dave and Clay decided to expand distribution in 2017 to regional markets, which also created more opportunities for their employees to grow.

"I like employing people. We've created opportunities for people to do what they love and for them to do new things and to grow and have new opportunities," said Clay proudly. "We're not a family business, but it feels like family."

"And at the end of the day, there's beer," smiled Dave, referring to the shift beer everyone gets.

"We rely on the people doing the jobs we used to do," recounted Clay, thinking back on the past ten years of Sun King and sixty-plus employees later. "We learned a lot about business in our first seven years, but in the last three years, we've learned a tremendous amount because Omar stepped back and retired. And Dave and I stepped up to literally run the company. Now it's like, 'Ahhhh! We run this whole thing,'" Clay said gleefully. "Oh," he continued more seriously, "*we* run this thing."

In 2019, Sun King produced thirty-two thousand barrels of beer, and it continues to win awards. It currently maintains four other locations aside from the main brewing facility downtown: the Small-Batch Brewery at The Yard in Fishers for innovative brews, a taproom and distillery in Carmel, a small-batch brewery in Kokomo and, most recently, a taproom at the Indianapolis airport. Plans are currently underway for more locations. The *Indianapolis Business Journal* consistently lists Sun King as one of Indy's top twenty most popular attractions. As of 2021, it is the second-largest brewery in Indiana.

Never in their wildest dreams did Dave and Clay think Sun King would be as successful as it's been. While Sun King continues to grow, locally focused, quality beer and giving back to the community have always remained at the core of their company values.

"People ask us all the time, 'Are you going to sell out?' My answer is, 'No, I've seen what it does,'" responded Clay, referring to witnessing what his father experienced. "We've had offers, and we could've taken truckloads of money, but at the end of the day, we both know that we started Sun

King because it's what we love and what we want to do. We didn't start this brewery to become rich—we started this brewery to follow our passion."

The sun began to rise as Clay walked to the brewery that morning, its warm glow peaking out from behind the brewery on College Avenue as he arrived to work to prepare for Sun King's ten-year anniversary celebration. It was still dark inside. Quiet. He entered the large, spacious taproom connected openly to the brewery. The sweet familiar scent of yesterday's mash still lingered in the air. He flipped on the lights as if to awaken the fermentation tanks standing like giants in the back of the room—freshly polished by the cleaning crew the night before. Clay lingered for a moment. Then Dave entered.

Clay turned over his shoulder and made eye contact with Dave. The two stood in quiet reflection, looking up at the fermentation tanks together. As if to extract and solidify the mutual thoughts of the moment, Clay took in a long, deep breath. He exhaled. "Wow. We did this…how the hell did we *do* this!?"

Moment of She

A loud scream pierced through the darkness at five o'clock that morning as Eilise Lane flipped the switch to begin milling the grain. The relentless breaking and snapping of husks and the sharp, slow cries of cracking kernels were hardly audible over the loud, persistent screeching of the grain mill. The dawn began to leer through the windows of the brewery. It spilled over the tall fermentation tanks, casting long, dark shadows over the cold concrete floors. A blood-red bandana tied up Eilise's ebony hair, painted with a streak of purple. She leaned over a steaming kettle of wort—a liquid that would soon age and transition into her famously beautiful Dorian Stout. The tempestuous scent of roasted coconut lured in the most beer-thirsty imbibers.

A gruff, bearded stranger entered the taproom that afternoon at Scarlet Lane Brewery, a brewery with a playful reputation for all things macabre. The stranger slammed down a pint of Vivian Red IPA. He scanned the brewery for someone in charge. He spotted Eilise's husband, Nick Servies, walking past. "You there!" he belted out. "What hops did you use in this IPA?"

Nick shrugged his shoulders. "I don't know," he responded, "ask her." He motioned toward Eilise, who stepped out from a steam-soaked cloud of grain dust. It glittered and danced and swirled up around her as she moved through the rays of sunlight now protruding into the brewery. Covered in grit and grim, her white polished nails remained pristine against her pink overhauls as she placed her hands on her hips.

"Yes, you had a question?" she said, waiting patiently.

Confused, the stranger muttered, "Well no…I mean…." he looked back at Nick. "I want to talk to your brewer."

"No, no, no," explained Nick, "*she's* the brewer. I like to make marketing stuff, and then if she tells me to go do something, I do it."

There was a time, ages ago, when women dominated the brewing landscape. A domestic chore, beer was a common household beverage, brewed for the home and for the community. As brewing evolved into a commercial endeavor, it became a man's world.

In 2007, Teri Fahrendorf took a road trip across the United States working as what she termed a "road brewer." During those collaborative brewing adventures, she connected with other female brewers. Many reported feeling isolated in a male-dominated industry, and some were unaware there even *were* other women in their profession. Fahrendorf became inspired. She founded the Pink Boots Society, a non-for-profit dedicated to supporting women in the beer industry, helping them connect and share information. They held the first meeting in 2008 at the Craft Brewer's Conference in San Diego, California. Twenty-two women attended.

By the time Eilise Lane opened Scarlet Lane in 2014, women brewers were still in the minority, especially in Indiana. Barbara Kehe was the first professional female brewer in Indiana. She began home brewing in the early 1980s. She worked as an assistant brewer at Back Road Brewery starting in 1997 and worked as a brewer at Duneland Brew House from 1999 to 2004. In 2013, she opened Ironwood Brewing Company in Valparaiso, making her the first female brewer in the state to open her own brewery.

In Indianapolis, there was Indiana native Tonya Cornett, who brewed at Oaken Barrel between 1999 and 2001. It was a challenge working in an all-male environment, but Tonya rose to the occasion. She left Oaken Barrel to attend the Siebel Institute in Chicago for brewing science and also attended the World Brewing Academy in Germany. In 2002, she pursued a successful brewing career at Bend Brewing in Oregon. Over the next ten years, she made quite a name for herself as the sole brewer and creative force behind the brewery's award-winning portfolio of beer. Tonya became internationally recognized for her brewing talents and inspired other women in the industry. She was the first woman to win the Champion Brewmaster

Cup that was awarded at the 2008 Brewer's Association World Beer Cup in San Diego. She won Small Brewer of the Year at the Great American Beer Festival that same year alongside Bend Brewing, which took home the Small Brewpub of the Year award. She's won several medals since.

There was Eileen Martin, who brewed at Fountain Square Brewery, as well as Upland Brewery in Bloomington and the Bloomington Brewing Company. Keely Thomlinson worked her way from assistant brewer at Alcatraz to brewmaster at Thr3e Wise Men (ironically), and brewmaster Liz Laughlin brewed some fantastic ales at Rock Bottom's College Park location. "Initially people were skeptical of my abilities," stated Liz in Holl and Schweber's book, *Indiana Breweries.* "They said, 'You're not very big.' And then they taste the beer and they say, 'Oh, I like this.'" Her kölsch and Simcoe India Pale Ale won best of show at the Indiana State Fair Brewers Cup competition. Then there's co-owner Holly Miller, who brewed in the beginning days of Black Acre Brewing. She developed the recipe for the now-famous Saucy Intruder Rye IPA. Many of these women have won prestigious brewing awards.

Anita Johnson homebrewed and taught others, owned and operated Great Fermentations and was a leader for Indiana's craft beer movement. There was Cari Crowe, who became the first female Cicerone in Indiana in 2014 and taught students about beer at Ivy Tech. She has worked in various industry roles and is currently the brewery sales representative at Daredevil Brewing. Julie Grelle was co-owner and president of the Circle V brewpub. She also taught "Introduction to Microbrewing" at IUPUI; helped form the Brewers' of Indiana Guild, where she served as secretary and treasurer; helped change Indiana's homebrew law; and founded and served as chairwoman for the Indiana Brewers' Cup competition. Grelle was an early voice representing women in Indiana's craft beer scene.

Sandy Cockerham is another name in Hoosier beer history and resides in Indianapolis. She is a scientist and began homebrewing in the 1980s. In 2019, she earned the distinct honor of becoming the highest-ranking woman judge in the Beer Judge Certification Program by reaching the level of Grand Master VI. She recently informed me, as I was writing this book, that she is now Grand Master VIII. Perhaps she will have reached the next level by the time this book is published.

Then there's the grande dame and Indiana beer legend Rita Kohn. As a beer writer (among many of her accolades) and one of Indy's original "craft beer evangelists," Rita has meant so much to the local craft beer community. She's worked tirelessly, building it up, singing its praises and always checking in on everyone. In 2017, Broad Ripple Brewpub and Scarlet Lane Brewery did a collaboration brew in her honor. Hangin' Tough was an oatmeal pale ale made with passion fruit and lemon. The label featured her likeness.

These were some of the first women engaged in the Indianapolis beer and brewing scene. What makes Scarlet Lane different—besides affinity for the macabre, 'round-the-clock Halloween decorations and its famous delivery hearse and coffin containing six taps for serving beer at festivals—is the brewery's focus on carving a space for women.

As the first female majority-owned brewing company in Central Indiana, it's made a mark on the craft beer scene, representing women in a beard-clad world. The main production facility lies just northeast of Indianapolis in McCordsville. As of 2019, there are an additional four locations serving Indianapolis and a total of about forty employees. She is the head brewer, owner, operator and CEO. She *is* Scarlet Lane.

"If I get hit by a bus tomorrow, Scarlet Lane will cease to exist," Eilise explained in our interview. "This is my life, this is my heart and soul, this is my blood."

The brewing bug bit Eilise during a two-and-a-half-hour road trip with her husband to Bend Brewing in Oregon. They lived in Eugene, Oregon, at the time. "It was a nice little trip over the mountain," she began. "We just wanted to have some food, have some drinks, kind of calm down and get out of [the] everyday."

It was an escape from her miserable job in Corporate America. She traveled a lot, working with new acquisition companies, finding a way to eliminate positions based on IT implementation. Her job was basically figuring out how to fire people because it was cheaper for the company. "It was so despairing," lamented Eilise. "People hated me. I was the grim reaper."

So, Eilise and Nick bellied up to the bar at Bend Brewing to unwind. She ordered a coconut stout. As she took her first few sips, she couldn't believe the flavors. It was sweet and rich, with notes of chocolate and toffee. "It just made me feel so good in that moment. There was something about that beer that spoke to me. I thought, 'I need to know who made this!'" she exclaimed. "Living in Oregon, the brewer is usually around, you know. So I asked the server, and they said, 'Sorry, she's not here today.'"

In that moment, Eilise's world turned upside down. She whipped around in disbelief. "*She*?!"

The server responded, "Yes, *she'll* be in tomorrow if you want to stop back by. Her name is Tonya." But they were leaving the next morning.

That night, Eilise tossed and turned in bed. *She…she…she* kept eating at her brain. All the brewers she knew at the time were men. Her restlessness kept her husband awake. He patiently listened as she tried wrapping her mind around the fact that this *woman* made this amazing beer. "[A]nd then two and a half hours in the car with me, through mountains, and he has to hear me, '*But it was this woman who made this amazing beer*,' and he's like, 'Uh huh, I get it.' So we pull into Eugene, and instead of going to our house, we go straight to Falling Sky Brewing Supplies. And he buys us our first homebrew kit."

Eilise brewed her first batch of beer on her kitchen stovetop. Nick helped but quickly decided that it wasn't for him. But Eilise? She fell in love. It became an obsession. When she wasn't firing people, she was firing up the brew kettle, making trips to the supply shop, visiting a brewery or spending time reading and learning all she could about brewing. Those were her moments of joy and levity:

> My parents and my husband finally sat me down and said, "This is the first time we've seen you happy in a long time. You're passionate. Why don't you do this?" I just kind of looked at them, dumbfounded like, "What!? No, you don't do this."…And then my husband very quickly pointed out that I had two stainless steel conical fermenters in our kitchen. You could no longer put cars in our garage…because I had put in a two-barrel brew system. I'd built a kegerator. I had three taps on at all times.

One day, a neighbor came over to barter eggs for beer. They lived in Whiteaker, a neighborhood where everyone barters with everyone, as Eilise described. People started asking for her beer on a regular basis. That's when she thought, *Maybe I* could *do this*.

Terrified of the unknown, she traded her corporate heels for pink boots and went back to school for fermentation sciences. During her studies, she began developing her now-famous Dorian Coconut Stout:

> I kept making little changes; a little of this, a little of that. Finally, I went down to the corner market and bought some coconut. I brought it home and I just, like, toasted a little bit of it…we'll see what that does. I started putting it in the beer—a little here, a little there…trying to figure it out. And then, Dorian Coconut was born. He is my baby and I love him.

Eilise also began volunteering at breweries as part of her quest to learn the trade and get her foot in the door:

"I will clean the stains on the floor if you promise you'll tell me something about what you're doing while you're brewing."…I can tell you that scrubbing the floor, cleaning tanks, kegging beer, transferring kegs from one of the taprooms to another taproom…wasn't sexy. There's a lot of physical labor, and there are moments of joy in it though because people are creating—people are artists. But it's also science. It's this wild, mad scientist artwork. It's something to really celebrate. And then you get to share that with people.

As Eilise worked her way into the brewing industry, she and a group of her peers attended the Craft Brewers Conference in Portland. The day spent learning industry trends preceded a fun brewer's cruise later that evening. While on the boat, enjoying a few pints, one of her friends ran from the lower level to the upper deck. Careful not to spill any beer, they approached Eilise. "Hey!" they blurted out, trying to catch their breath, "*Tonya* is down there!"

"*WHHAAATTT!?*" exclaimed Eilise.

"Yeah…Tonya from Bend Brewing!" Eilise froze.

"Just go talk to her. You're being weird," asserted her friends.

"No! I'm not being weird. I can't do this," protested Eilise. "This woman changed my life!…She has no idea how much meeting her would mean to me."

Finally, she worked up the courage to meet her hero:

Tonya was so shocked that she made an impact in my life. I don't cry a lot, but I cried because talking to her was a good moment—to meet someone who is fantastic and as amazing as I wanted her to be. She was really down to earth and really cool. So we're sitting and we're chatting on this boat. She's from Indiana, and we both live in Oregon. It was really weird how many times we'd crossed paths. I felt like I was in the right place at the right time. I've been wildly lucky that the woman who brewed that beer has been introduced in my life in a lot of different ways.

Eilise later got the opportunity to work with Tonya on a collaboration beer:

She's brilliant. Now, if I'm stuck and I can't figure something out, I text Tonya, "Help me I can't figure this out!" Or, "Where can I buy hibiscus right now?" She's always there to help. It's been really great that the woman who created a beer that completely changed my entire life has been able to be with me in my mental capacity back then, but right now in a real way. My hero is now one of my friends. And we're both Hoosiers.

Since the beginning of Scarlet Lane, Eilise continues looking for ways to support other women:

That's not to say I don't love my male counterparts and the male folk, but I do think there are certain times where you want to look and say, "Let's find a way to find more women that are going to be in the industry." I think the most recent study said that 7.5 percent of head brewers are female. That's a shocking number that just mystifies me. How is that even possible? There could be more—there should be more.

Eilise spoke of her experiences as a woman in a traditionally male-dominated industry:

It's a weird challenge I've had actually. I have a lot of men who work with me, for me at the brewery, and it's always the first question goes to them: "Oh, hey man, so I'm here to install this, what do I do?" "Ask her." "Uh…the girl?"

There are times, and it has happened to me recently, where I will sit down and grab a beer and the bartender will try to talk me out of the beer I ordered. So even something as slight and small as that could give a woman cause to think, "Well, I don't know what I'm talking about even when ordering a beer. So why am I going to trust myself to go into this industry?" But then some women, it makes them go, "Oh, no, I do want that Russian Imperial Stout and go get the Bourbon one too…let's go!" And others will be like, "Maybe you're right. Maybe I would be happier with having a white zinfandel or something."

One evening, Eilise had a girl's night out with the Ladies of Beer, an informal group of brewery owners and head brewers and women who work with beer groups directly. They decided on a night of cocktails and settled on a place where no one would know them so they could let loose. It was a super big girly night full of sequins, hair, nails, lipstick and glitter. Someone from a beer bus party saw the ladies walk into the bar. They approached the girls and began pontificating to them. "Well, if some of these breweries would actually cater to women," they said, "and they can make really nice fruity beers…if you'd be interested, we could find something that would be easy for you to drink."

Shocked, the ladies responded, "Well, what kind of beer do you think we'd want?"

We played into it to find out what people were saying out there. After he found out we were beer professionals, I could tell it made him really uncomfortable and he apologized.

It's just things like that. And that's why we should probably have a few more women out there that are visible. So people are aware that there are other women out there doing this. Where men don't make the assumption that just because I go out and I have on sequin and glitter that I don't know what I want.

It's difficult, but I hope in some small way I'm helping break the stereotype. So I hope if there's someone out there that sees, "Oh, the head brewer at Scarlet Lane is a woman?" And they have that same lightbulb moment I had at Bend Brewing, that moment of she. I think that helps. It's opening the eyes of the ability that you can do this. This is something that is meant for you too.

Today's Craft Breweries

Sun King set the gears in motion for Indy's modern-day craft brewery scene in 2009. Early breweries were rugged and industrial—and I don't mean in the sense of design aesthetic. It was function over form. Basically, breweries were like, "Hey, we're making beer and you can come on in and have some, maybe we'll throw up some chairs…maybe some used couches." Most were located in off-the-beaten-path industrial complexes—concrete floors, bare walls, florescent lights. Enthusiastic volunteers poured beer behind a table usually consisting of three to five different taps as people noisily asked questions. Nearly everyone brewed a pale ale, accompanied by an amber ale, a porter or stout, an IPA and a wheat beer.

The first batch of breweries after Sun King were like pillars for Indy's budding craft brewery scene. Bier Brewery opened in 2010. Jerry and Darren Conner, a father-and-son team, started on a bootstrapped system with a fifty-five-gallon brewing capacity. They quickly made an award-winning name for themselves on what they describe as "little more than a glorified homebrew system." The first beer they canned was Weizengoot, a German hefeweizen; followed by PDG, an American pale ale; and their German-style Special Kolsch. They currently keep this core lineup, as well as rotating IPAs and seasonal brews.

That same year, Sean O'Conner founded Flat12 Bierwerks, derived as a combination of his passion for auto racing and a discovered love of German and Belgian beers during his time living and working in Europe. Cofounders included Rob Caputo and Steve Hershberger. Sean was a finance executive with an expertise in operations, Rob had more than fifteen years' experience as a homebrewer and became the head brewer and brewing director, and Steve was a marketing technology and social media specialist. They opened the brewery in Indy's Holy Cross neighborhood, just east of downtown in an area formerly home to German immigrants. Flat-twelve is a type of twelve-cylinder engine used in the sports car racing of yesteryear. Sean formed a relationship with famed IndyCar driver James Hinchcliffe. The two collaborated on a pilsner called Hinchtown Hammerdown. Flat12 was also known for its Pogue's Run Porter, named for Indy's urban creek that is named for George Pogue, one of the city's first white settlers. Flat12 quickly grew. In less than three years, it became a multi-state supplier. In 2019, new owners acquired the brewery and rebranded as Rad Brewing Company. It closed during the COVID pandemic.

Business partners David Waldman and brewer Jon Lang opened Triton Brewery in 2011. It's located at historic Fort Benjamin Harrison in a former mule barn used more than one hundred years ago by the U.S. Army. Triton launched its flagship ales such as RailSplitter IPA and Deadeye Stout, which continue to be best-sellers.

Fountain Square Brewery began brewing in September 2011 with reclaimed equipment from the Alcatraz brewpub, which had closed earlier that year. Skip Duvall, who was head brewer at Alcatraz, joined the new brewery. Founders included a team with backgrounds in science and technology. Bill Webster was a microbiologist and avid homebrewer and Jeff Gibson a chemist. They worked together at Eli Lilly. Bill's neighbor Justin Brown worked in electrical engineering technology and had a familiarity with the craft beer scene. He helped automate some of the brewing and bottling processes. They used their combined knowledge to produce consistent, quality beer with increased shelf stability and were one of the first breweries in Indianapolis with a dedicated yeast lab.

Jon Lang, brewer (*left*), and David Waldman, founder (*right*), at their eighth anniversary. *Triton Brewery.*

The trio also had a love and appreciation for the arts. Wanting to be part of the neighborhood's growth, they opened in the then up-and-coming Fountain Square Cultural District, known for its retro vibe and arts scene, and utilized their taproom space to host local artists and musicians. They hosted their grand opening in January 2012 with a big Winter Luau celebration. Core beers include Workingman's Pilsner, Preacher's Daughter Amber Ale, Hop for Teacher Pale Ale, Soul Ride IPA and Backyard Porter.

Black Acre Brewing opened its doors that same year. It started on a modest three-barrel system in Indy's historic Irvington neighborhood along the old National Road. Steve Ruby, Justin Miller and Jordan Gleason, three of the founding owners, attended law school together. Matt Johnson and Holly Miller were also founding members. Beers like Saucy Intruder and Natural Liberty drew naming inspiration from legal cases. The name Black Acre comes from a legal term used as a placeholder to reference a hypothetical piece of land. "The real moment of clarity for me," stated Gleason to the *Indianapolis Star*, "was when we were picking hops in Justin's backyard, and Steve mentioned how much more fun this was than practicing law."

The year 2013 brought Indiana City Brewing to the Home Brewing Company's old bottling plant. The next year saw Scarlet Lane, Books and Brews, MashCraft and Chilly Water. Jason Wuerfel's big heart for community and affinity for books led him to open the city's first and only bookstore-meets-brewery. Books and Brews, "a place for people without a place," soon grew into a local franchise with beers named after literary works.

Andrew Castner opened MashCraft in Greenwood and later locations throughout Greater Indianapolis. Skip Duvall, from Alcatraz and Fountain Square Brewery, founded Chilly Water from his love of craft beer and passion for music. He eventually sold his shares to his head brewer and former Fountain Square Brewing comrade, Dan Krzywicki. Chilly Water continues as a music-focused brewery, hosting local musicians and naming beers with clever song title puns. It brews mostly top-quality, classic lagers, paving a road in an ale-driven craft beer society.

The days of small, artisanal breweries have made a comeback. Passion has converged with the art and science of brewing. A great sense of community over competition has helped the craft beer scene flourish. Each brings his or her own ideas to the table. Many produce innovative brews, representing Indiana as their reputation grows across the nation.

Upland Brewing Company in Bloomington has been around since 1998, inspired by the rugged, rolling hills of the Indiana Uplands. It opened a small tasting room in 2009 in Indy's SoBro neighborhood. Its

Jason Wuerfel at Books and Brews. *Amy Beers.*

outdoor adventure–inspired core lineup includes Campside Pale Ale, Dragonfly IPA and Bad Elmer's Porter. It also brews an Indiana-historic, pre-Prohibition lager called Champagne Velvet, originally brewed by Terre Haute Brewing Company.

In 2006, Upland did something no other craft brewery in Indiana had yet done. It began experimenting with sour ales after trading a few cases of beer for a few wine barrels from the local Oliver Winery. Now, in addition to its regular house beers, it has a dedicated sour production facility called the Wood Shop. Upland has since expanded to several locations, including another in Indy's Fountain Square Cultural District. It continues innovating and expanding its sour program as a leading producer of Belgian-style sours and wood-aged wild ales.

While Upland brewed Belgian-style sours, another brewery approached Belgian-style ales from a different perspective. Taxman opened in 2014 in Bargersville, Indiana. It has since expanded and operates three farm-to-table gastropubs, including the most recent CityWay in downtown Indianapolis. Through the years, it has earned a reputation for its acclaimed Death & Taxes Day, an outdoor beer release and tasting festival.

Three of Taxman's four founders are tax professionals and include husband-and-wife team Nathan and Leah Huelsebusch. Before founding the brewery, they lived in Belgium for tax consulting work. There, they became inspired by the country's beer culture, as well as the beer itself, with its complexities and depth of flavor. They spent an extensive amount of time in research to bring a taste of Belgium back to their Indiana home.

Taxman offers a wide range of Belgian-inspired ales that often utilize local ingredients for a midwestern twist on Belgian classics. Its diverse portfolio includes American farmhouse ales, Midwest saisons and a substantial cellar program where it produces small-batch wine and spirit-aged beers, as well as sour, wild, funky ales.

Where many early brewers led with a focus on English-style ales like the pale ale and the porter, Upland and Taxman introduced the local craft beer community to something different, each in its own unique way.

As competition grew, so did the need to stand out in a crowded marketplace. Branding and marketing played a greater role as breweries considered the entire craft brewery experience: brewery image, design and aesthetics, social media, messaging and mission statements, as well as the products themselves. They looked for ways to differentiate themselves from other breweries.

One such brewery, Deviate, opened in 2015 with the guiding mantra to "deviate from the norm." By this time, the craft beer scene, and palates, had become well established. Before the extreme craft beers and milkshake IPAs of today, owners and brewers Greg Ortwein and Mike Orkey crafted creative concoctions like Rye Chipotle Porter and Watermelon Mint Ale.

St. Joseph, Daredevil, Blind Owl, Wabash and Big Lug Canteen breweries also opened in 2015. St. Joseph Brewery converted the dilapidated St. Joseph Catholic Church in Indy's downtown Mass Ave Cultural District into a space for good beer, food and fellowship. The beautiful interior and unique location, with brewing activity at center stage, pays homage to the tradition of monks who brew in the monasteries. It's kept the religious theme with beers like Confessional IPA, Absolution Amber and Prophesy Porter.

Daredevil Brewery originally opened in Shelbyville in 2013 with the launch of Lift-Off IPA, a West Coast–style American IPA. Award-winning craft brewers Bill Ballinger and Michael Pearson, along with craft beer enthusiast (and Michael's twin brother), Shane, founded the brewery. Demand for their beer grew quickly. Out of necessity for a bigger facility, they moved near the Indy Motor Speedway in 2015. They later expanded to Daredevil Hall in 2019 in the Nora neighborhood of Indianapolis. Their vision was to be "recklessly daring," as they were not afraid of a challenge and were willing to take educated risks. Lift-Off IPA continues to be one of the best-selling craft beers across Indiana.

A local restaurant group opened Blind Owl Brewery as a typical neighborhood bar and grill. What wasn't typical, however, was the brewer it hired. I remember my first visit to the brewery, where I met a twenty-two-year-old Alex Petersen. We struck up a conversation over my tasting flight. With a beaming smile, he proudly informed me that he was the youngest head brewer in the country. After graduating from Butler University, and before the age of twenty-one, Petersen called up every brewery in the state, hungry to learn the trade. Omar Castrellon took the young lad under his wing at the now-defunct Thr3e Wise Men Brewery. He soon became head brewer at Blind Owl, where he introduced patrons to his passion for German-influenced brews.

Wabash College friends Damon Carl, Matt Kriech and Nic Stauch founded Wabash Brewing with a nod to all things Wabash-related. 503 Amber Ale was one of their first brews, perfected from their early homebrew days. (503 is the length in miles the Wabash River runs from its source near Fort Recovery to its outflow into the Ohio River.) Their blonde ale, Waapaahsiiki, is a tribute to the Miami Nation, whose territory included the Wabash River. Cannonball Pale Ale hints to an 1882 song about a fictional train with connections to Purdue and Indiana State, both located along the river.

Indy's restaurant royalty created Big Lug Canteen. A few years later, Liter Haus and Half Liter BBQ and Beer Hall followed in tandem. The Sahm family empire began when Ed Sahm opened his first Indianapolis restaurant in 1986. His son, Eddie Sahm, along with his business partner and brewer, Scott Ellis, wanted to create a different type of brewery aesthetic—one that stood apart from what they deemed the "hyper-masculine wooden beer dungeons" that so often dominated the look of breweries at the time. Big Lug opened in Nora with bright, fun, vibrant colors and a welcoming beer garden next to the Monon Trail. A trip to Germany inspired a Bavaria-meets-Indiana brewpub concept. In 2018, Eddie and Scott opened Liter Haus. Shortly after, they opened Half Liter, a conjoining German beer garden and Texas BBQ smokehouse. This Germany-Indiana-Texas mashup is nestled along the Monon, located about five miles south of Big Lug via the Trail.

Metazoa Brewery opened in April 2016 near Indy's Fletcher Place neighborhood. Ever since day one, it has donated a portion of its profits to various animal and wildlife foundations. Beers like Hoppopotamus IPA and Puppy Slumber Party peanut butter milk stout reflect the animal theme. It often works with the Indianapolis Zoo on special releases to help raise money for conservation efforts. Brewmaster John Hall came to Metazoa after a long career in brewing that included a position as head brewer at Goose Island in Chicago. He and Nick Betzner, head brewer and director of brewing operations, lead a fantastic team of brewers. Metazoa has won many awards for its beer. In 2021, it was recognized as Brewery of the Year by both the Great American Beer Festival and the Brewers' Cup. It is the only brewery in Indianapolis with a dog park and hosts regular adoption and fundraising events. Since opening, it has earned a reputation as Indy's animal brewery. Owner, homebrewer, animal lover and beer enthusiast Dave Worthington shares a collection of old Indiana brewery bottles in the entryway display. The brewery recently expanded into a facility built in 1905 that once housed a baking and confectionery equipment manufacturing company. Metazoa began production there in April 2022, adding pre-prohibition-style lagers to its portfolio. It's fittingly located near the zoo.

The year 2016 also saw openings of Centerpoint Brewing and Black Circle Brewery. Centerpoint opened in the Circle City Industrial Complex near Woodruff Place—Indy's first suburb. Award-winning homebrewers and Rose-Hulman Institute of Technology graduates Jonathan Robinson, Peter Argiris and Jeff Ready founded Centerpoint. Their backgrounds in engineering drive their meticulous attention to detail, with the mantra "precision-engineered craft beer for everyone."

Black Circle is the brainchild of former bank employees and homebrewers Jesse Rice and Dan Gayle. Noticing a void in the craft beer community, they founded the brewery as a music and event venue. It's located in the Refinery 46 Industrial Complex on the fringe of Midtown and South Broad Ripple in a former grocery warehouse. They regularly host live music that includes everything from metal to rock and bluegrass. The name Black Circle is a reference to the record. When they're not hosting live music, they are almost always playing music on vinyl. Black Circle is also known for its comedy and drag shows. Its small, three-barrel operation puts out quaffable beers like Skeleton Key Porter and Pixel Punk Pale Ale and seasonal ales like Hail Santa. Recently, it expanded down the road to Loom. The chill 1990s basement vibe includes a bar, a remote office and meeting spaces, as well as a coin-operated laundry facility.

Indy's craft beer scene continues to expand. The latest additions include the Mayfair Taproom, Garfield Brewery, Traders Point, Guggman Haus and 18th Street Brewery, and the newest addition, Kismetic, opened as this book was in the editing phase.

John Hill's son, Alec Hill, continues the family legacy at the Mayfair Taproom near Woodruff Place. Originally built in 1895, the space housed many businesses throughout the years, including a pharmacy, barbershops, a library, the Mayfair Tavern from 1935 to 1985 and a bar called Mustang Sally's, which closed in 1999. John and his wife, Nancy, purchased and remodeled the building. The Hills transformed the decade-long vacant space and opened the Mayfair Taproom in 2018. Alec and his wife, Hilary, manage the operation.

Garfield Brewery opened that same year on Indy's Southside near Garfield Park. Before it became a friendly neighborhood craft beer spot, it housed a Texaco service station through most of the mid-century and, after that, a small diner called Sister's Place in the 1980s. The building sat vacant for more than twenty years. Ted Herrera, a former brewmaster at Terre Haute Brewing during the 1990s, is part owner of the neighborhood brewery, along with his son Kyle, Gary Kinnett and Larry Agresta. With help from locals, they name beers in honor of the neighborhood. Hervey Street Hefe, St. Catherine Sienna Lager, Red Line American red ale and Friday in the Park American ale are a few examples. They created their tap handles from reclaimed pews from the neighborhood's former St. Catherine's church.

What began as a family homebrew hobby turned into a full-fledged business while still juggling full-time day jobs. A labor of love, Trader's Point Brewery opened in 2018 near Zionsville. Its mission is to simply serve quality-driven beer and contribute to its community in a positive way. Beer names are subtle nods to family members. The Traders Truck, a teal blue 1963 Ford Econoline pickup, has become a neighborhood icon.

The Guggmans, as they've come to be called by combination of their last names, opened Guggman Haus Brewery as an extension of their homes in 2019. Identical twin sisters Courtney Guggenberger and Abby Gorman and their husbands, Derek and Ryan, began developing the concept for their brewery in 2015. The Guggenbergers' inspiration came from time spent living in Germany and the Gormans' from time discovering the craft beer culture in Denver, Colorado. The family's spirit of adventure and exploration pairs with a heart for community and talent for hospitality.

A most unique aspect of Guggman Haus is its location at the old Boyle Racing Headquarters. The Guggmans joined with vintage racing enthusiasts who had formed a foundation with Indiana Landmarks to help save and honor a piece of Indianapolis racing history. They spent years renovating

Guggman Haus Brewery. *From left to right*: Derek and Courtney Guggenberger and Abby and Ryan Gorman. *Michael Durr Photo/Video.*

Billy DeVore (*left*) and Wilbur Shaw (*right*) drink beer after a race, 1933. *Indianapolis Motor Speedway.*

the former garage that was once home to three-time Indy 500 champion Wilbur Shaw, owner Mike Boyle and other famous drivers and mechanics. One of the original brick walls remains. It is now part of the brewery's large taproom and event space. The building also includes a Boyle Racing memorabilia shop.

A few of Guggman's house beers pay tribute to Indy's racing legacy. Wilbur's Prize Pils is a nod to Wilbur Shaw. His love of automobile racing and dismay over a dilapidated Speedway that was abandoned during World War II prompted Shaw to enlist the help of Terre Haute businessman Tony Hulman. Hulman purchased the tired and deteriorated Indy Motor Speedway. Shaw came on as president and general manager. Together, they helped revive the "Greatest Spectacle in Racing."

Guggman's Winner's Milk Jug milk stout is named for an Indy 500 tradition where the winner of the race drinks milk. The tradition dates back to 1936, after Indy 500 winner Louis Meyer drank milk from a large glass bottle at Victory Lane. An executive of the Milk Foundation saw a photograph of the event in the next day's newspaper. Excited by a marketing opportunity, he vowed to make sure the winner's milk jug became a tradition.

In February 2020, 18th Street Brewery opened a taproom in Indianapolis, shortly after *USA Today* honored it as the best brewpub in the country. Drew Fox started his home brewery on that street in 2010. Three years later, he opened 18th Street in Gary, Indiana, with a mission to prove himself, challenge the city's notorious reputation and break through its stereotypical assumptions. The brewery launched with the release of Sinister DIPA. He quickly outgrew that location and expanded to Hammond and, later, to an underserved neighborhood in Indy.

Historically, the brewing industry and consumers of beer alike have predominantly consisted of the white male population. Those demographics, however, are shifting. As the first Black-owned brewery owner in Indiana, Drew Fox helped paved the way for a more inclusive and equitable industry. Backstep Brewing in Crawfordsville and Hop River Brewing Company in Fort Wayne Indiana opened in the wake. Many area breweries participated in the nationwide "Black is Beautiful" collaboration campaign in 2020 to help bring awareness to the injustices that many people of color face daily and to show that the brewing community is an inclusive place for everyone of any race. Nonprofit organizations, such as Chicago-based Black and Brew, founded by Mickey Bryant, work to educate, promote diversity and build bridges for underrepresented demographics, including women and the

LGBTQ community. Diversity Ambassador Sahera Syed recently organized an Indianapolis chapter.

The craft beer landscape is dynamic and ever-changing. Some Indianapolis breweries have come and gone, while others, like the Kismetic Beer Company, opened most recently. Owners Nicole Oesch and her husband, Ryan, followed their dream after working together at a local brewery where they met. Nicole worked as the brewery's taproom manager and then sales director, managing the wholesale team and private events. Ryan started as a bartender and worked his way to production manager. The name Kismetic, which is a combination of *kismet* and *kinetic*, speaks to the idea of moving toward and manifesting your destiny. Nicole draws on her past experiences to run and manage the taproom, while Ryan focuses on brewing. Black Circle helped them get started, allowing use of its equipment in the beginning for a collaboration brew. Kismetic officially opened in April 2022 in the 201 Studios artist complex with a strong sense of community. The two collaborated with local creative studio Guide and Anchor to help design the visual brand and aesthetic. Bicursal Designs helped with the physical buildout and Owens and Crawley with detailed touches, including handmade decorative tiles. The chic 1970s vibe—with wood paneled walls, posh velvet curtains, reclaimed vintage furniture and lighting fixtures, engraved decorative mirrors and a stone façade reminiscent of a fireplace, complete with a hanging woven tapestry of the brewery's logo that stands behind the bar at center stage—is a welcome addition to Indy's craft beer scene.

There are also the breweries in the Greater Indianapolis region and extensions of long-established breweries sprinkled in places from north in Carmel to south in Greenwood. Hoosier, Planetary and SmockTown Breweries are within walking distance of one another in Old Town Greenwood. There's Urban Vines, Field Brewing and Grand Junction Brewing in Westfield. Noblesville has Primeval and Barley Island Brewing Companies. Four Day Ray resides in Fishers. Located in Carmel are Union Brewery, Danny Boy Beer Works, Fork and Ale House and Flix Brewhouse and movie theater. There are many others to explore.

BEYOND THE GRAVE

It was back. "Someone must be playing a trick on me," thought Indiana City Brewery owner Ray Kamstra as he used his foot to wipe away the "X" strategically sketched in the layers of dust on the old wooden floorboards of the abandoned second story. It was the third time the "X" mysteriously appeared in that same exact spot. No one else had been up there.

This wasn't the only occurrence of unexplained supernatural activity at Indiana City Brewery. Several staff members have reported their personal experiences inside the brewery once occupied by the Home Brewing Company's bottling plant—a rush of cold wind when no doors or windows are open, unexplained banging and clanging noises when no one else is in the building, the creaking of footsteps and the gentle wisps of distant voices.

One brewer noticed fresh, wet footprints created from a boot much larger than his. He was the only person in the building that morning. A different day, as he poured beer from a tap, he felt the sudden urge to get out of someone's way, as if someone were trying to sneak past behind him in the narrow passage behind the bar. He looked. No one was there. An employee once heard an argument between a man and a woman. Again, no one else was in the building. Another brewer witnessed a bucket fly up from a table and crash with force against a wall before falling to the floor—almost as if someone, or *something*, picked it up and threw the bucket in a fit of rage. "Before we even opened, we had a contractor who'd been working late hours on the build out process," explained Ray as he gave me a tour of the building. "He eventually refused to work late hours because he kept telling me too many things were happening that spooked him out. At first I just shrugged it off, but turns out he may have been telling the truth!"

The building that houses the Indiana City Brewery is the last standing testament to Indianapolis's brewing history—marked from an era of brewing giants dismantled by Prohibition, left to be forgotten in the dust.

As Indiana signed Prohibition into law, the Home Brewing Company sent a letter to its customers. The end came with this statement: "[T]he day will dawn again in Indiana, when a man can drink what he wants, when personal liberty will again be a citizen's right." The Home Brewing Company had closed its doors by 1920—like a nail in a coffin, a cork in a bunghole.

More than one hundred years later, in 2012, homebrewing enthusiast Ray Kamstra serendipitously found himself connected to a place cellared in time. The sun was just beginning to grace the presence of Lady Victory's torch that morning. She looked out on Indianapolis from her post high above atop the Soldier's and Sailor's Monument.

Ray set out that morning in search of an industrial space in a centralized location for his microbrewery. He wanted it to be as close to downtown as possible, which was a challenge. At first, nothing really called to him.

Then he saw a tire shop for rent on Shelby Street, south of Washington and Southeastern Avenue. "It was basically a plug-and-play brewery. It had floor drains, tall ceilings, a loft for grain, high voltage electricity, air compression. It had everything I needed to get started as a small brewery," explained Ray. "But unfortunately, it was way out of our price range."

Sometimes disappointment leads to better opportunity. The sun beamed fully now through the clouds that afternoon. Ray turned around to discover a "For Sale" sign directly across the street. The building was abandoned, surrounded by a barbed wire fence. All the doors and windows were shuttered. The interior was dark, collecting dust. The lot was overgrown with weeds, waiting for a passerby to notice, for someone to breathe life back into the once-glorious bottling plant of the great Home Brewing Company.

Ray felt the old brick building call to him and stepped inside. He looked around at the high ceilings, wood rafters, the steel, the columns, the exposed brick and the concrete. It had everything he needed for a brewery. In that moment, he knew that it was meant to be.

Ray experienced his first craft beer in 2003 at a tiny bar when he lived in Boston. It was Dogfish Head's IPA. "It blew my mind that there was a local brewery making this great beer," he exclaimed.

Then he moved to Chicago to study graphic design at Columbia College, which progressed into working as a creative director in brand management. During this time, he discovered neighborhood breweries like Half Acre and Revolution Brewery, and Metropolitan Brewery was located just a few blocks from where he lived. This newfound access to a variety of craft beer, as well as befriending some of the brewers, greatly influenced him. He began homebrewing as a hobby.

Ray continued his hobby after he moved back home to Indianapolis. Eventually, he wanted to take it a step further and open a craft brewery. His skills and background in branding and marketing, combined with his love for beer and brewing, naturally led him to the decision. Over the years, he's had his hand in almost every aspect of the business:

I really saw beer as the perfect opportunity to combine two things that I really enjoy doing. To me, visual art is a big part of craft beer. The best breweries have great beer but also have the best artwork. It's the full experience. Each can is an opportunity for a fresh new canvas. I can't take credit for anything we've put out art-wise though. We have an amazing artist, Aaron Scamihorn, who helps bring ideas to reality. Then there's the Craft Brew Doodle Crew that he started. It's a group of local artists. They work on labels in a collaborative, musical chairs type manner. Each individual label is a joint effort.

The time had come for Ray to take his hobby to the next level. He met with the building owner. The two negotiated. Instead of buying, Ray worked out a lease agreement. An opportunity to freshen up the space lay just ahead—a blank canvas.

"What are you going to use it for," asked the owner.

"A brewery," answered Ray.

"You won't believe it," he said, "but this place used to be the bottling plant of the Home Brewing Company." Unaware of its history, Ray was pleasantly surprised. He signed the contract.

November was move-in date. For the next six months, Ray and his team set to work resuscitating the tired, old space. Light poured into the room as, one by one, they opened all the doors and windows shut tight to the world for years. A gust of cold winter air rushed in through the broken remains of the paned glass windows. Hammers and nails echoed in the hollowed spaces as the construction team framed out the walls. Brewing equipment clamored its way into the production room as the plumbers and electricians finished up the last of their work. They installed the draught system—a handful of taps ready to pour beer.

Indiana City Brewery's first guests and supporters arrived to the grand opening in May 2013, just in time for Indy's big race season. The Home Brewing Company had formed with the help of stakeholders. Similarly, Indiana City raised $35,000 in startup capital in thirty days with help from the community through a Kickstarter campaign. "We had all this local support right out of the gate," explained Ray, "but when we announced the history of the building in the middle of that, it really got people to look a little harder and see what's happening here."

While Indiana City isn't trying to re-create the historic Home Brewing Company, the parallels existing between them are uncanny. Ray's start was in homebrewing. The Home Brewing Company's philosophy carried a spirit familiar to craft beer today—locally brewed beer for the community. The name "Indiana City" and "Home Brewing" allude to the idea of place and sense of community. The original logo Ray designed, before being privy to the Home Brewing Company's logo, turned out very similar. Both logos represent Lady Victory's torch, and the flames of both blow in the same direction. There's also the fact that the Home Brewing Company held a

Ray Kamstra, Indiana City Brewery. *Amy Beers.*

competition for local artists to design the brewery's logo; Ray employs the help of local artists in their beer label designs.

Perhaps something *did* call to Ray the day he discovered the abandoned bottling plant—a thread that connected the past and the present. A force from beyond the grave, beckoning Ray to continue a legacy in the last remaining relic of Indy's brewing history.

Two different ghost hunting organizations, on two separate occasions, have paid visits to the brewery. Both reported a ghost named Albert. Could it be the ghost of Albert Lieber? Old age and Prohibition forced Lieber to retire, and he never did like competition. Perhaps the supernatural activity experienced at Indiana City Brewery is the ghost of a once-famous brewing giant, still trying to maintain control over Indy's brewing industry. Is it unfinished business? Is Albert Lieber still with us, throwing buckets against the wall in frustration?

Perhaps there is something at work in the depths beyond what can be seen with the human eye. The next time you're visiting Indiana City Brewery, keep an eye out for that "X." Maybe it's marking a spot—a portal between time and space.

Appendix

INDIANAPOLIS BREWING HISTORY TIMELINE

KEY BREWERIES, PRE-CRAFT BEER ERA

"The Indianapolis Brewery"
The first commercial brewery in Indianapolis opens on Maryland Street.

Wernweg & Young

1834-1867

Christian Frederick Schmidt establishes a brewery with Charles Jaeger at McCarty Street. In 1863, Jaeger leaves to establish City Brewery.

C.F. Schmidt

1850/1867-1873

1859-1920

Casper Maus begins brewing in 1865 and forms Casper Maus & Co. In 1868, he establishes the C. Maus Brewery at West New York and Agnes Streets.

C. Maus Brewery

1864/1871-1932

A group of local investors form the Home Brewing Company. Officers include August Hook and William P. Jungclaus.

The Home Brewing Company

1865/1868-1902

1890-1931

1891-1920

Meikel's Brewery

The city's first successful brewer, John P. Meikel, begins brewing in 1850 at the Indianapolis Brewery. In 1867 he transfers his brewery to the Washington Street location.

P. Lieber Brewing Co.

Peter Lieber and business partners purchase City Brewery in 1864. In 1871, he moves his brewery to the Madison Avenue location.

The Indianapolis Brewing Company

The Schmidt, Lieber and Maus breweries merge and incorporate as the Indianapolis Brewing Company. Albert Lieber becomes president.

Joseph Charles Schaf opens the American Brewing Company. He is the first native-born to establish a brewery in Indianapolis.

The American Brewing Company

1897-1918

1905-1915

Indiana enters Prohibition in 1918. Repeal comes in December of 1933.

PROHIBITION

1918-1933

The International Brewing Company and General Brewing Corporation merge to form the Gold Medal Brewing Company. Efforts are made to restore the old IBC's Lieber plant.

Gold Medal Brewing Company

1933-1936

1933-1935

Indiana Breweries, Inc. reincorporates as the Indianapolis Brewing Company, Inc. in 1936. The Bardin Brothers purchase the brewery in 1945. They close after a tax evasion scandal and short-filling bottles.

The Indianapolis Brewing Company

1933-1937

1936/1945-1948

Capital City Brewing

Capital City Brewing is established. Officers include Charles Krauss, John J. Geisen and Victor R. Jose.

Indiana Breweries, Inc.

Leo C. McNamara establishes Indiana Breweries, Inc. in the old Indianapolis Brewing Company's Maus plant.

Richard Lieber Brewing Corp.

Colonel Richard Lieber buys into the Midwest Brewing Co. (established the same year) and renames it the Richard Lieber Brewing Corp. and later the Lieber Brewing Corp.

BIBLIOGRAPHY

Books

Baer, Teresa M. *Indianapolis: A City of Immigrants*. Indianapolis: Indiana Historical Society, 2012.

Bakken, Dawn E. *On This Day in Indianapolis History*. Charleston, SC: The History Press. 2016.

Beers, J.H. *Commemorative Biographical Record of Prominent and Representative Men of Indianapolis and Vicinity*. Chicago: J.H. Beers & Company, 1908.

Bodenhamer, David J., Robert G. Barrows and David Gordon Vanderstel. *The Encyclopedia of Indianapolis*. Bloomington: Indiana University Press, 1994.

Brown, Ignatius. *Logan's History of Indianapolis from 1818*. Indianapolis, IN: Logan & Company, 1868.

The Cyclopædia of Temperance and Prohibition: A Reference Book of Facts, Statistics, and General Information on All Phases of the Drink Question, the Temperance Movement and the Prohibition Agitation. UK: Funk & Wagnalls, 1891.

Dunn, Jacob Piatt. *Greater Indianapolis: The History, the Industries, the Institutions, and the People of a City of Homes*. Vols. 1–2. Chicago: Lewis Publishing Company, 1910.

Geib, George W. *Indianapolis: Hoosiers' Circle City*. N.p.: Continental Heritage Press, 1981.

Holl, John, and Nate Schweber. *Indiana Breweries*. Mechanicsburg, PA: Stackpole Books, 2011.

Bibliography

Hyman, Max Robinson. *Hyman's Handbook of Indianapolis: An Outline History and Description of the Capital of Indiana.* Indianapolis, IN: M.R. Hyman Company, 1897.

———. *Journal Handbook of Indianapolis: An Outline of History.* Indianapolis, IN: Indianapolis Journal Newspaper Company, 1902.

Indianapolis Illustrated: The Capital City of Indiana: Its Growth, Resources, Commerce, Manufacturing Interests, Financial Institutions, and Prospects, Also Sketches of the Leading Business Concerns Which Contribute to the City's Progress and Prosperity: A Complete History of the City from Foundation to the Present Time. U.S.: Consolidated Publishing Company, 1893.

Kohn, Rita T. *True Brew: A Guide to Craft Beer in Indiana.* Bloomington: Indiana University Press, 2010.

Leeds, Marc. *The Vonnegut Encyclopedia: An Authorized Compendium.* UK: Greenwood Press, 1994.

Manufacturing and Mercantile Resources of Indianapolis, Indiana: A Review of Its Manufacturing, Mercantile and General Business Interests, Advantageous Location, &c, to Which Is Added a Historical and Statistical Sketch of Its Rise and Progress. N.p., 1883.

Nowland, John H.B. *Nowland's Early Reminiscences.* Indianapolis, IN: Sentinel Book and Job Printing House, 1870.

———. *Sketches of Prominent Citizens of 1876.* Indianapolis, IN: Tilford & Carlon, 1877.

One Hundred Years of Brewing: A Complete History of the Progress Made in the Art, Science and Industry of Brewing in the World, Particularly During the Nineteenth Century. U.S.: H.S. Rich & Company, 1903.

Ostrander, Bob, and Derrick Morris. *Hoosier Beer: Tapping into Indiana Brewing History.* Charleston, SC: The History Press, 2011.

The Oxford Companion to Beer. New York: Oxford University Press, USA, 2012.

Pictorial and Biographical Memoirs of Indianapolis and Marion County, Indiana: Together with Biographies of Many Prominent Men of Other Portions of the State, Both Living and Dead. U.S.: Goodspeed Brothers, 1893.

Salem, F.W. *Beer: Its History and Its Economic Value as a National Beverage.* Hartford, CT: F.W. Salem & Company, 1880

Shields, Charles J. *And So It Goes: Kurt Vonnegut: A Life.* New York: Henry Holt and Company, 2011.

Smith, Gregg. *Beer in America: The Early Years, 1587–1840: Beer's Role in the Settling of America and the Birth of a Nation.* Boulder, CO: Siris Books, an imprint of Brewers Publications, 1998.

Smith, Oliver H. *Early Indiana Trials and Sketches: Reminiscences*. Cincinnati, OH: Moore, Wilstach, Keys & Company, 1858.

Sulgrove, Berry R. *History of Indianapolis and Marion County, Indiana*. Philadelphia, PA: L.H. Everts & Company, 1884.

Vonnegut, Kurt. *Palm Sunday: An Autobiographical Collage*. New York: Random House Publishing Group, 1981.

Wissing, Douglas A. *Indiana, One Pint at a Time: A Traveler's Guide to Indiana's Breweries*. Indianapolis: Indiana Historical Society, 2010.

Directories

Indianapolis City Directory Collection. IUPUI University Library, Digital Library. https://www.ulib.iupui.edu/digitalcollections/icd.

Journals, Articles and Essays

Bennett, Pamela J. "The Indiana Historian." Indiana Historical Bureau, June 1996.

The Chamber. "Activities" (1926).

Hedeen, Jane. "The Road to Prohibition in Indiana." Indiana Historical Society, Indianapolis.

Hofman, Mike. "The Great Beer Crisis of 2008." *Inc. Magazine*, n.d.

Indiana Magazine of History 67, no. 1. "Richard Lieber and Indiana's Forest Heritage" (March 1971) 45–55.

Indiana Magazine of History. Indiana University–Bloomington, Department of History, Indiana State Library, Indiana Historical Society. Bloomington, Indiana, 1913.

Journal of Wine Economics 10, no. 3. "Craft Beer in the United States: History, Numbers, and Geography" (2015): 242–74.

Lerner, Michael. "Prohibition." PBS. https://www.pbs.org/kenburns/prohibition/unintended-consequences.

O'Sullivan, Mary A. "Yankee Doodle Went to London: Anglo-American Breweries and the London Securities Market, 1888–92." *Economic History Review* 68, no. 4 (November 2015): 1,365–87.

Paulsen, Monrad. "Natural Rights: A Constitutional Doctrine in Indiana." *Indiana Law Journal* 25, no. 2 (1950).

BIBLIOGRAPHY

Newspapers

Daily Journal.
Daily State Sentinel, Indianapolis.
Indianapolis Business Journal.
Indianapolis Journal.
Indianapolis Monthly.
Indianapolis News.
Indianapolis Star.
Indiana State Gazette.
Indiana State Sentinel.
NUVO.

Websites

Encyclopedia of Indianapolis Online. https://indyencyclopedia.org.
Price, Nelson. Hoosier History Live: Natural Gas Boom of 1880s and '90s. https://hoosierhistorylive.org.
U.S. Department of the Treasury, Alcohol and Tobacco Tax and Trade Bureau. "Historical Tax Rates." https://www.ttb.gov/tax-audit/historical-tax-rates.
Wikipedia. "C.I. Taylor." https://en.wikipedia.org/wiki/C._I._Taylor.
———. "Indiana Gas Boom." https://en.wikipedia.org/wiki/Indiana_gas_boom.
———. "Indianapolis ABCs." https://en.wikipedia.org/wiki/Indianapolis_ABCs.
———. "Indianapolis in the American Civil War." https://en.wikipedia.org/wiki/Indianapolis_in_the_American_Civil_War.
———. "Indianapolis Union Station." https://en.wikipedia.org/wiki/Indianapolis_Union_Station.
———. "The Propylaeum." https://en.wikipedia.org/wiki/The_Propylaeum.

General Internet Resources

http://hoosierbeergeek.blogspot.com.
http://indybeersleuth.com.
http://www.18thstreetbrewery.com.

BIBLIOGRAPHY

http://www.mayfairtaproom.com.

http://www.twentytap.com.

https://blackacrebrewing.com.

https://daredevilbeer.com.

https://drinkin.beer.

https://hooksmuseum.org/our-history.

https://indianaontap.com.

https://lafbrew.com/about.

https://nlbemuseum.com/history/players/taylorc.html.

https://sabr.org/bioproj/person/c-i-taylor.

https://terrehautebrewingcompany.com/history.

https://townepost.com.

https://tritonbrewing.com.

https://www.ale-emporium.com.

https://www.bierbrewery.com.

https://www.blackcirclebrewing.com.

https://www.brewersassociation.org.

https://www.broadripplebrewpub.com.

https://www.centerpointbrewing.com.

https://www.craftbrewingbusiness.com.

https://www.greatamericanbeerfestival.com.

https://www.guggmanhausbrewing.com.

https://www.homebrewersassociation.org.

https://www.in.gov/library.

https://www.indianabeer.blogspot.com.

https://www.indianapolismotorspeedway.com.

https://www.metazoabrewing.com.

https://www.slipperynoodle.com.

https://www.sunkingbrewing.com.

https://www.taxmanbrewing.com.

https://www.thepropylaeum.org/history-of-the-propylaeum.

https://www.turkeyrunstatepark.com/turkey-run-state-park-history.

https://www.worldbeercup.org.

https://www.youarecurrent.com.

BIBLIOGRAPHY

Interviews with the Author

Casey, Kwang, Oaken Barrel. June 8, 2021.
Colt, Dave, and Clay Robinson, Sun King Brewing. July 31, 2019.
Cornett, Tonya. E-mail correspondence.
Hill, John, Broad Ripple Brewpub. January 21, 2020.
Johnson, Anita. August 9, 2020.
Kamstra, Ray, Indiana City Brewing. October 6, 2020.
Kehe, Barbara. E-mail correspondence.
Lane, Eilise, Scarlet Lane Brewing. August 21, 2019.
Smith, Ron. August 4, 2021.

Other

Beebe v. The State. 6 Ind. 501. Supreme Court of Indiana, December 1855.
Congressional Record: Proceedings and Debates of the…Congress. Washington, D.C.: U.S. Government Printing Office, 1952.
Dunn, Jacob Piatt. *Indiana and Indianans: An Index*. Indianapolis, IN: Indianapolis Public Library, 1919.
Noland, Stephen C., editor-in-chief. "Nowland Family Records and Oral History." Citizens Historical Association, Indianapolis, IN. http://www.plainfieldlibrary.net/wp-content/uploads/2015/03/Nowland.pdf.
Reports of Cases Decided in the Supreme Court of the State of Indiana. Vol. 6. Indiana Supreme Court, 1890.
Richard Lieber Papers. Indiana State Library.

INDEX

U

Union Brewery 37, 43, 48, 137,
    172
Union Station 23, 29, 58
Upland Brewing Company 64,
    126, 156, 164, 165, 166
Urban Vines Winery & Brewery
    172

V

Vojnovich, Mark 125

W

Wabash Brewing 166, 167
Waldman, David 162
Wernweg, William 26
Wernweg & Young 27, 28, 37, 138
Wildcat Brewing Company 125
Wright, Frank 36, 37
Wuerfel, Jason 164

Y

Young, John L. 26

ABOUT THE AUTHOR

Amy Beers lives up to her name. Ms. Beers is an Indiana native and a Certified Cicerone® (a beer sommelier) living in Indianapolis. She owns and operates a beer tour company called Drinking with Beers that offers an enriching experience for beer and history lovers alike. A graduate of Indiana University, she obtained a Bachelor of Arts degree in mass communications and film studies. This is her first published book. More of her work may be found at drinkindianahistory.com, as well as her social media channels. You can also find her on YouTube. Amy is an avid world traveler. She loves to hike, explore, visit museums, learn about different cultures and gain new perspectives. If she were granted one wish, it would be to travel back in time. In a sense, writing *Indianapolis Beer Stories* has allowed her to do so. She is excited to share this experience with you.

THE BIRTH OF JESUS